P9-CAB-045

God made me Beauty-full

Building Self-Esteem In African American Women

Terri McFaddin

Quiet Time Publishing
P.O. Box 10366
Marina del Rey, CA 90295

Copyright © 1997 by Terri McFaddin

Quiet Time Publishing
P.O. Box 10366
Marina del Rey, CA 90295

Library of Congress Cataloging-in-Publication Data
McFaddin, Terri
        God Made Me Beauty-full/Terri McFaddin
        1. Title
Library of Congress Catalog Card Number 97-65701
ISBN 1884743 056

Cover Art: *"Phenom"* by Paul Goodnight © 1995
Cover design: Wayne Dailey
Editors: Toni Mathews/Stephen Sweeney/Nicole' Johnson

All rights reserved, including the right of reproduction which must have written permission from the publisher except by a reviewer who may quote passages in a review.

All scripture references in this book are taken from "Holy Bible, New King James Version" copyright © 1988/Broadman & Holman Publishers and The Living Bible © 1971, Tyndale House Publishers, Inc. All rights reserved.

2 3 4 5 6 7 8 9 10 11 12 printing

A QTP/Balance Project

In memory of
My mother
Barbara Louise Prunty

My grandmother
Sadie Bell Campbell

My great-grandmother
Shelly Jones

My great-great-grandmother
Cordelia Jones

Special Acknowledgments

To God be the glory for the things He has done!

Cover art entitled "Phenom"
Charcoal 29.5x41 - by Paul Goodnight

A very special thanks to my dear friend, renowned artist Paul Goodnight for the use of the charcoal rendering entitled "Phenom." His paintings appear in galleries, television and movie sets across the country. He also served as the official artist for the 1996 Olympics. I am truly blessed to have him as a brother and a friend. For information regarding limited editions of "Phenom," call or write:

> *Color Circle Art Publishing, Inc.*
> *791 Tremont Street - Suite #N 104*
> *Boston, Ma. 02118*
> *(617) 437-1260*

Graphics and cover design by Wayne Dailey
Dailey Communications.
Thank you for giving me your very best.

A special thanks to Ruthann Rountree, B.A., M.S.W., M.Div. for her guidance in making this book possible.

A special thanks to Pastor Andrae' Crouch and the Christ Memorial Church family.

Contents

Introduction

As far back as I can remember I have always loved to fix or restore things that have been broken or discarded. When I was twelve years old my family moved from a third floor apartment in West Philadelphia into our first new house in a suburb called Germantown. When the pickup truck arrived at our new address my mother proudly stepped on to the sidewalk with her hands on her hips and a big smile on her face.

"Well, this is it!" she said introducing us to our new home. My brother and two sisters stared in disbelief as they got a closer look at 69 W. Johnson Street.

The porch was almost falling down, the windows were broken, the paint was badly chipped and the yard looked like a jungle. But as I studied my mother's face, I knew that she could see something that nobody else could.

"Are we going to fix this place up?" I asked.

"Love can fix almost anything," she said escorting us through the front door.

In the months that followed, we rebuilt the front porch and sanded the oak floors. Dad argued that we were trying to do too much too soon. Mom agreed but we kept on working. With the little money that we could scrape together we plastered, painted and made new curtains for the windows.

With a lot of love and hard work the big old Victorian house and everything inside of it was gradually transformed into something beauty-full to behold. It simply took someone who could see the potential beneath the badly neglected exterior.

It is the memory of that beauty-full house that compels me to look for the beauty in people, even when it is buried beneath the rubble of deception or neglect.

God Made Me Beauty-full is a declaration of self-acceptance based on the knowledge that we are made in the image and likeness of a flawless and awesome God. The word "beautiful" defines that which is stimulating, yet superficial and temporal. In contrast, "beauty-full" defines that which reflects the glory and the gifts that emanate from the inner chambers of the body, soul and spirit. Each time an African-American woman discovers her true beauty and value, it lifts all African-American women to a higher level of self-acceptance.

It is my prayer that the contents of this book will help you discover the fullness of your beauty. If any part of that beauty has been disrespected, damaged or discarded, it is my hope that you will be renovated, repaired and restored into the powerhouse that you were meant to be from the beginning.

* * *

Thoughts of Suicide

Life.
Will it ever get any better?
I cry.
I weep.
I always wonder, why me?
I look around and see smiles and laughter,
But all I feel is pain.
I feel, all it will take is one bottle of sleeping pills,
and a cool glass of water.
Then I can be with Jesus.
He would never put me down.
He would never tell me I am ugly.
He would wipe my tears, and kiss my fears.
He would rock me in the cradle of His arms.
Jesus would never call me a failure or disrespect me.
He would never be ashamed of me.
I would never have to be afraid
of being laughed at or made fun of.
I can be pretty,
because my outside body would perish.
In heaven I can be me, the me hiding inside.
I would never cry again.
Why should I have to live in a world where there is no love?
My father has a kingdom filled with love for me,
and filled with angels ready to hug me and comfort me.
Why should I live?
Why?

TIFFINE L. GRIFFIN Age 16   10-27-95

Tiffine stared at the floor as I read her poem. Her skin was like smooth dark chocolate. Her hair was short and slightly unkept. Her full lips drooped down and were slightly parted, like she had something to say, but no one to really listen.

Behind her glasses, her eyes were dark and inquisitive, yet sad. I knew she had a thousand questions, but maybe she would feel stupid, if she asked.

Tiffine was tall, at least 5'10." Her arms and hands were long and powerful. A mountain of hips and buttocks protruded from her curvaceous back. Strong muscular legs carried a set of perfectly formed, wide, thick feet.

Her movements were smooth and fluid like a gazelle walking along a river's edge. It was clear to me that she could have mastered any sport. And as I read her poetry, I could only imagine the many gifts that might be hiding in this young woman who was so full of sorrow that she wanted to die.

Tiffine's brush with suicide began with an abusive boyfriend who controlled her by making her think that she was so ugly and worthless that no one in their right mind would want to be with her. He constantly compared her to White or Hispanic women who had long hair and light or white complexions. To make matters worse, when he was angry, he used demeaning words to make her feel like she was nothing. With no one in her life to tell her otherwise, Tiffine began the downward spiral that almost led to her destruction.

Even though Tiffine's story is somewhat extreme, many women of color have been systematically robbed of their sense of beauty and value by painful encounters inflicted by a society where dark skin and coarse hair have a negative view. This takes precedence over the gifts and talents on the inside.

Tiffine followed me to my office. I reached for a big book with a picture of Africa on the cover and began to turn the pages.

"So what do you think of Michael Jordan?" I asked.

"He's great!" Tiffine answered. I continued to turn the pages of the book revealing pictures of smiling faces of the men and women of Africa.

"How about Shaquille O'Neal. Do you like the way he looks?"

"Yeah," Tiffine smiled at me for the first time.

"Have you ever seen his mother?" I asked.

"No!" Tiffine frowned. She was lost and couldn't imagine where I was going.

"She's tall, over 6 feet. She's dark, with a nose and mouth just like yours. If Michael Jordan and Shaq are beautiful in your eyes, then how can you not see the beauty in the women who gave them the power and grace that made them champions?"

It was clear that the wheels of her mind were beginning to turn. Tiffine stared at the picture of an African woman dressed in a beautiful bright yellow dress with a matching yellow and gold headpiece. Her broad hips seemed to gyrate as her wide, thick, feet danced to the music of the drum. The woman's skin was like polished ebony. Her thick, burgundy lips curved into a broad grin revealing a set of perfectly carved, ivory white teeth.

"Her feet look like they're bigger than mine," Tiffine said, still studying the picture.

"Do you think she's pretty?" I asked looking over her shoulder.

"No!" Tiffine smiled. "She's not pretty... *she's the most beautiful person I have ever seen!*"

"And you look just like her," I whispered in her ear.

Tiffine continued to study the pictures, amazed at the pride and dignity that emanated from the beautiful women of Africa.

On the following Sunday I saw a young lady that I did not recognize sitting in the seat that was formerly occupied by

Tiffine. She was tall, with coffee colored skin. Her hair was braided into a crown on the top of her head. She wore bronze eye shadow and a soft shade of ruby lipstick. Later in the service the girl came forward for prayer.

She was wearing a beautiful dress with an African accent. As she came closer I could see it was a transformed version of Tiffine. She held her head high and walked erect as she passed the pulpit. I smiled at her and she winked back as she headed to her seat.

What had transformed this sad and insecure young woman? She simply discovered her true identity. Her beauty and value as a member of the human race had suddenly been redefined. She was no longer in bondage to a false perception of herself. At last she could be proud of her size, her shape and her color.

"Can you imagine how awesome my children are going to be?" she said with a big grin.

* * *

All women of color, who have grown up in America have, to a certain degree, been infected with the dreaded disease of self-hatred, brought on by a malicious propaganda that says we are God's big mistake. Therefore, we don't deserve the best educational opportunities, the best jobs, the best homes, or the best men.

In spite of all the progress we have made, the demons of racial hatred and abuse still torment us. If we go shopping, there is the false perception that we might steal what we could never afford to purchase. Behind every successful Black man there's a White woman spending his money and living large. Behind every Black woman are the children she is raising, without the assistance of a husband or a father.

In reality, the spectrum of Black women is very broad

and includes: The Afro-centric sister sporting her dredlocks, nose ring and worshipping her ancestors. On the other end of the spectrum is the Black woman who is wrapped up in a Euro-American image and lifestyle. She feels more comfortable working and living in a "safe" cosmopolitan environment. In between, there's a mixture of Women's Lib'ers, high profile Lesbians, Muslims, New Ager's, college girls, and welfare mothers. If you turn in any direction you will find African-American women in search of an identity that will give them back the dignity and courage essential to their survival.

Discovering the truth about your racial heritage can give you a new lease on life. But racial identity is only the beginning of the journey. We need a deeper revelation in the discovery of the beauty-full woman inside. We were fashioned and created in the image of God. He is our maker. Therefore, we cannot truly appreciate and understand ourselves until we come to know our Creator. Discovering the Living God is the doorway to self-discovery.

* * *

Mirror Mirror on the Wall

"Mirror, mirror, on the wall, who's the fairest of them all?" Most of us know this quote from Snow White and the Seven Dwarfs. The answer to *who's the fairest of them all?* is important to a woman's self-image, but there are more important questions that should be directed to the image in the mirror. *"Who am I? What is my value? What is my purpose in life?"*

How you answer these questions will determine the quality of your interpersonal relationships, your career goals and your spiritual life.

In the esteem building class that I teach, I took out a mirror. Yolanda, who was sitting next to me, smiled nervously as the small mirror was passed around. Each woman looked at their reflection, as I spoke words that affirmed their beauty.

"God said we are fearfully and wonderfully made, so let's rejoice in our creation," I said. When the mirror was passed to Yolanda, I noticed that she took a quick glance and passed the mirror to me, like it was burning her hands.

"Did you really take a good look at yourself?" I said handing her the mirror again.

"I don't like looking in the mirror," Yolanda replied looking very uncomfortable.

"Why would a beautiful woman like you dislike looking at yourself?" I asked.

"Because I'm ugly!"

The whole class looked at her with shock and surprise. Yolanda is so strikingly beautiful. She is a mixture of American Indian and Black. Her smooth, light brown complexion and long black hair complimented her chiseled features and big, dark brown eyes perfectly.

"What makes you think you're ugly?" I asked.

Yolanda took a deep breath, then began to tell us the painful story of how she grew up. Her mother, who is a full blooded American Indian, had an affair with a Black man and soon found that she was pregnant. By the time Yolanda was born, she and her mother were considered family outcast. Her mother was called "the loose woman with a n____ baby".

As Yolanda grew into a little girl, she soon became the target of her mother's hurt and bitterness. "All my life I was called an ugly little n____ girl," Yolanda wept.

To make matters worse, even though Yolanda was normal and very bright, her mother enrolled her in a school for the mentally retarded to get extra money from the state. When the teachers protested, her mother forced them to keep her in the school. By the time Yolanda reached her teens she was reading on a second grade level.

Yolanda left home at sixteen, and through sheer determination, she managed to get an education. Later she became the manager of a computer design firm. Although she has found healing for a lot of the damage that was done to her, the small hand mirror that sat on the table, made it evident that she had not been healed from a damaged self-image.

While it is true that many women who come from racially mixed backgrounds have found love and acceptance, there are those who have grown up in environments where they have been ostracized and abused for being partially Black or for not being Black enough. A woman can have an Irish mother and Italian father and be considered Irish/Italian; she can have a German father and Chinese mother and be considered German/Chinese; but with one drop of Black blood, she is just another Black woman.

The moral of Yolanda's story is: Never assume that a person's self esteem is in tact just because she is attractive, successful or wealthy. Once the mirror of a woman's self-image has been broken, no matter how beautiful she is, the reflection is always full of distortions.

The premise of this book is to help you discover your beauty as an African American woman. This discovery can only happen when women of color see themselves as their Creator sees them... a perfect design - fearfully and wonderfully made.

Because of the details and complexities involved in the creation of the universe, it is clear that the color of our skin and the texture of our hair was not a cosmic accident. God had a precise plan for every inch of our external and internal creation.

We were created a living body, soul and spirit. *Our bodies are specifically designed to compliment the gifts and talents that are hidden in our souls.* The plan for our lives is communicated through the vehicle of our spirit.

Jackie Joyner-Kersee's flaring nostrils and wide mouth might have caused her to be a confused, young Black woman heading for the nearest plastic surgeon to get a nose job. But God had a perfect plan. He made Jackie's nostrils and mouth wide enough to take in enough oxygen to set three Olympic records.

Unfortunately, most people have a preoccupation with physical appearance. But how we look only constitutes a small part of who we are.

God made us *Beauty-full* and *full-of-beauty.* We are "full" of gifts and talents that cannot be seen with the natural eye, and those same gifts will make room for us and bring us before kings. God has a plan and purpose for us that is *Wonder-full* and *full-of-wonder.* The plan is designed to make our lives *meaning-full* and *full-of-meaning.* Once we discover the layers and depths of our inner-beauty, then we can accept our differences, because they are what make us the unique person that God intended us to be.

Only 10% of our beauty is visible to the eye. 90% of our real beauty is hidden on the inside.

The challenge with many African American women is that they live as if 90% of their beauty is on the outside for everyone to see. And only 10% of their beauty is on the inside. In reality it is the vast domain of inner beauty that brings radiance to our outer person.

But what does beauty on the inside look like?

Beauty-full Spiritually: This woman loves God. She studies and lives by His principles. Her trademark is that of being kindhearted, forgiving, dedicated, prayerful, and self-controlled. She dedicates herself to serving God, her family and community. This woman's spiritual beauty comes from her desire to maintain a high standard of moral excellence in her life-style, even when under pressure to conform to the world's system.

Beauty-full Gifts and Talents: This energetic woman is constantly discovering her gifts and talents, and uses them effectively. She focuses on the vision that she has for her life. She takes the time to be a teacher and a mentor to those who are following in her footsteps. This beauty-full woman does not covet the gifts and talents of others. She learns how to use her own gifts effectively by serving others. She is a gold mine of talents. She can be found in music or art; flying airplanes or repairing cars. Politics, ministry, business, medicine, or designing new technology are swirling around in her genes waiting for the time when her special gifts and talents will be used for the good of all mankind.

Beauty-full Personality: What is more refreshing than a woman who is comfortable just being herself? She may be funny, outgoing, lovable, caring and generous. She stimulates the people around her with her sense of adventure, energy and positive attitude. On the other end of the spectrum, another beauty-full woman may be a home body who is quiet, gentle, a good cook and a good listener. She too is considerate, helpful, supportive and always full of encouragement. Her beauty shines through as she demonstrates care and concern for her friends, family, the poor and needy, and the young and old.

Beauty-full Character: She can be trusted with the possessions of others and with personal and sensitive information. Her courage and tenacity cause her beauty to shine even brighter. She is dependable, highly productive and supportive. She is a hard worker and not afraid to get her hands dirty, or to serve others. Her character shines through the words of wisdom and encouragement she readily showers on others. She never speaks lies or uses deceptive, profane words. She is discreet and careful to avoid the very appearance of evil. She is trustworthy, honest, loyal, faithful and sincere. All of these characteristics can be found in the heart of the beauty-full woman.

Beauty-full Intelligence: This woman gives a clear and consistent demonstration of wisdom and understanding. She makes good decisions and knows what should be done and how to do it. She is constantly seeking new training and greater knowledge. She is full of creative ideas and witty inventions. This beauty-full woman has integrity and humility. She is skilled at knowing how to perform a task without being arrogant. She is not afraid to train and reproduce her skills and abilities in others. This woman loves the challenge of solving problems, whether they be in the home, the workplace, her community or church.

All of the beauty-full attributes listed above cannot be seen with the natural eyes. Just as you groom yourself on the outside to look attractive, it is important that you make an investment in the development of your inner-beauty.

* * *

Out of Africa

How many women look into the mirror on a daily basis with an unrelenting assault against their own bodies?

The ritual begins with:
- My nose is too big.
- My lips are too thick.
- My hair is too short or too coarse.
- My skin is too dark, blemished, oily or dry.
- My breasts are too small or too big.
- My butt is too big.
- My stomach is too round.
- My thighs are too thick.
- My legs are shaped funny.
- My feet are too wide.

It is important to understand that it is the male gender who sets the standard for validating a woman as beautiful or condemning her as unattractive. In most cultures of the world the father figure is the first one to validate his daughters beauty and value. He esteems her by providing for her and protecting her until a suitable male comes along with a proposal of marriage. When it is time for a woman to marry, again the man, to a great extent, has the privilege of selecting a bride. Because men are aroused by visuals, physical appearance plays a big part in his selection. It is for this reason that women put so much time and energy into hair, clothing, diet and cosmetics.

Unfortunately, for the African women who came to America in chains, it was the slave traders who placed their naked flesh on the auction block and became the supreme judge of their beauty and value. Based on their perverted standard, they made bids. The value of a female slave was based upon youth, shape, attractive face, solid teeth, good health and disposition.

The White trades placed a high value on the beauty of ebony colored African women if they had full buttocks, strong legs and wide feet. The names they were given showed the delight and admiration of the White masters. They gave these women names like "Big Pearl," "Ruby" and yes, even "Sapphire." Although these names are now viewed in a negative light, they are a clear indication of the value that was placed on slave women of African descent. Unfortunately, the need to control them was more important than the need to show admiration. Therefore, Black women were valued as property, not human beings.

It is important to understand the fine art of how one human being controls another. The slave traders began with physical control. This was accomplished with superior weapon power. African spears were no match for guns and cannons. Once physical control was established, our captors had to establish mental control. This was accomplished by creating fear and self-hatred in the mind of the African slave. Just as an abusive husband tells his beautiful wife over and over that she is ugly and worthless to keep her in mental and emotional bondage, so the slave masters set out to completely destroy the self-esteem of the slaves. Black skin became the badge of disgrace, while White skin was viewed as the embodiment of all that was good, clean and valuable. When a person or a group of people are called dirty, worthless and stupid for a long period of time, the effects cause lasting damage to the soul and spirit.

As the practice of slavery became more sophisticated and more racial mixing occurred, the value system changed. Female slaves who were mixed were considered more attractive, therefore more valuable. Another important factor that created a higher value in mixed slaves was the fact that they were the offspring of the White slave masters. This created a bond between slave and master.

Mixed slaves were divided into three categories. The top of the line was the OCTOROON, which was one-eighth Black blood. Some Octoroons passed for White and married or became the mistress to White men. The QUADROON was one-quarter Black blood. She frequently lived in the "big house" working as a house servant or a personal maid or nanny to her White mistress. The MULATTO was one-half Black blood. She too shared many of the same privileges of her Octoroon and Quadroon sisters.

The darker full blooded African women with strong bodies were forced to work in the fields and perform heavy labor. They lived in subhuman conditions and survived off of the scraps of food that were given to them. Pregnancy was no escape for the tortures of slavery. They had their babies while working in the fields. All too often they miscarried or died.

It is because of this painful heritage that the color line still runs deep among African-American women. Many Black women are still in bondage to the idea that women with lighter skin are more desirable than women with darker skin.

In spite of the seemingly privileged life of young and attractive female slaves, in reality it was the women who were considered physically attractive who suffered the most. Historians have uncovered the unspeakable horrors of rape and other types of sexual abuse that African-American women were forced to endure. One obscure story is told of a pretty slave girl who had not yet reached her teens. Her master entertained his male guests by laying the girl on a table and allowing the men to rape her. She died prematurely due to the physical trauma to her underdeveloped body. Another story is told of a jealous wife who waited for her husband to leave the plantation on a business trip. While he was gone, she ordered a mulatto slave girl to be beaten to death for sleeping with the master.

The male counterparts were used for breeding and as house servants to entertain guests. The lighter the complexion, the more delicate the features, the silkier the hair, the greater the value.

Unfortunately the issue of skin color and hair texture has remained a stronghold among many African Americans. Phrases like *"Good Hair"* and *"Fair Complexion"* continue to reflect the bondage of self hatred that is both archaic and ignorant. In some circles, hair that is wavy or straight (a trait that comes from racial mixing) is considered "good hair." In reality, if you have any hair at all, that's good. "Fair skinned or fair complexion" refers to a Black person who is light or nearly white. The term "fair" refers to that which is lovely, pleasant and good. The fact is, that anyone with nice skin, regardless of the color, has "fair" skin!

* * *

African American men have also been haunted by the ghosts of slavery. A Black man who is tall, has a muscular body, and drives a nice car, may be a lawyer, but White people will inevitably ask, "are you a professional athlete?"

Before we were emancipated, male slaves were judged

by their size, muscle mass and strength. The prized "studs" were used for mating to produce strong offspring. They were also used for labor in the cotton, sugar cane and tobacco fields. Male slaves were also used in a variety of sporting events. Plantation owners would stage boxing and wrestling matches as well as foot racing events using the best of their male slaves. The smaller sized Africans were used as horse trainers and jockeys. They were small, but power-full. They graced the winner's circles of Derby's all across America and even in Europe. To this day, statues of Black jockeys can still be found decorating front lawns across the country.

African slaves brought a wide variety of talents and crafts to the plantations, farms and businesses across America. They designed and hand-crafted furniture. They were also instrumental in the design and construction of the great mansions of the south. In Africa, they made weapons and tools from iron. This same craft was used to create large decorative gates and staircases made by the hands of African iron-smiths. The women were skilled quilt-makers and also designed clothing for their mistresses. They also understood herbs, medicine and became trained nurses and midwives. Hundreds of inventions, which were credited to Whites, in fact, came from the minds of Black slaves. Those who were skilled craftsmen or athletes were sold at a high premium on the auction block.

It is regretful that many of the standards that were used by slave traders still prevail today. African-American athletes who have the size, strength and muscle mass still go to the highest bidder. Women with lighter complexions and silkier hair are still often viewed as more attractive. Men of all colors dream of being in a romantic escapade with Vanessa Williams or Halle Berry, while Whoopie Goldberg and Nel Carter are only good for laughs.

It is also important to note that once slavery was abolished, many of the slaves did not know where to turn. It was the friendly Indian tribes who came to their rescue by allowing them to join their ranks. This accounts for the wavy hair textures, keen features, high cheek bones and red complexions found in many African Americans. To a great degree, when it comes to the American Indian, we are without a doubt "first cousins."

* * *

In the mid-sixties, the National Association For The Advancement of Colored People (NAACP) took a survey of Black children to determine how they felt about their color. They had the Black children choose between a White doll and a Black doll. Almost all of the children chose the White doll, because they saw it as more beautiful and desirable when compared to the Black doll.

On a personal note, I can still remember my youngest sister Lillian receiving a Black doll for Christmas. That night when she was taking a bath, she put the Black doll in the tub with her. She thought by washing the doll, the dirty, brown color would go away and the doll would be "clean and white."

Her actions were certainly understandable when you consider the fact that the images of beauty we were exposed to as children were all White women. There was "Snow White" (what a metaphor), "Cinderella" and "Sleeping Beauty." I can even remember the "Breck Shampoo girl," her silky blond hair blowing in the breeze and her bright blue eyes sparkling in front of the camera.

African-American women and men have been in a constant struggle to keep a strong sense of their true value and worth. For hundreds of years, we have been ridiculed for our color, hair, features and intelligence. During the 1930's, Al Jolson painted his white face black and became famous for singing a song called "Mammy," which was degrading to

Blacks. During the 1950's, the Amos and Andy television show featuring the infamous Sapphire and her Momma perpetuated the myth of Blacks as ignorant and ugly. During the 1970's, a show called "Good Times," continued the assault. The family members were poor, unattractive, uneducated and always having problems.

The blood of our African-American forefathers cries out from the soil of the nation that they labored to build. The truth is simple and profound.

The infamous "Middle Passage" made us the powerfull people that we are. The Middle Passage refers to the transporting of slaves from Africa to the Americas. The trip from Africa meant no less than five to twelve tortuous weeks of being buried in the rat infested hull of a ship, lying in bodily waste, with no space to move, very little air, food, or water and the rapid spread of disease. John Newton, who wrote the famous hymn "Amazing Grace... that saved a wretch like me," was referring to his guilt ridden life as a slave trader. Watching the diseased bodies of slaves being thrown overboard to waiting sharks, brought him to a place of such tremendous shame that he gave up slave trading and accepted his call to the ministry.

The Africans who survived long enough to stand on the auction blocks were living proof that they were men and women who had been endowed by God with superhuman physical, mental and spiritual strength. These were our ancestors. If you are ever feeling weak and powerless, just remember that the blood of the "Middle Crossing" flows through your veins. You are a survivor... you are an overcomer.

Any men and women strong enough to survive the crossing indeed would be a threat, yet at the same time they would be an asset to slave masters. This has been the deep seeded fear that White Americans have carried over the years... the spiritual conviction, the physical strength and the mental fortitude of the African-American is certainly not to be taken lightly.

South America, North America and Europe could not have flourished without the African people. Muslim slave traders were the first to introduce the Europeans to the powerful Africans. During the 1400's, the Portuguese began their raids on West African fishing villages. Later they manipulated warring tribes into selling their hostages in exchange for guns and other European goods. But the strong male prisoners of war were of little value without the power-full African women who could produce children.

African-American women should never feel inferior! The names of famous African women like Cleopatra, Bathsheba, Nefertiti, and the Queen of Sheba still echo through the corridors of time. African women are so awesome that men came from around the world to capture over 20 million Black women. White men braved tropical diseases, wild animals, hostile warriors and steaming jungles in search of what they called "Black Gold."

It was the superior strength and beauty of Black people that built nations. The full buttocks, muscular arms and legs and wide thick feet were the very features that gave us the power to endure the abuse of slavery. White men fought wars to possess our ancestors. Yet, we were lied to and made to believe that we were ugly, lazy and worthless. How could a people that worked and died to build a nation be lazy? How could a people who produced George Washington Carver, Dr. Charles Drew, Madame C. J. Walker, Martin Luther King, Maxine Waters, Maya Angelou, Stevie Wonder, Michael Jordan and Oprah Winfrey, ever be considered worthless.

The truth is that we were cherished more than all the gold and diamonds on the African continent. We have always been the most powerful and productive men and women on this planet. Babies still flow from our wombs like ripe fruit replenishing the earth with the gifts of music, art, science and literature.

* * *

One of the greatest challenges of overcoming the effects of slavery is the danger of taking on the characteristics of the oppressor.

People in bondage quickly learn to hate and fear the one who is oppressing them. But deep inside they come to admire the power of their oppressor. All too often when the ones who are being oppressed are liberated, they will emulate the people who oppressed them. This gives them a false sense of power and acceptance.

The flamboyant Dennis Rodman, who plays basketball for the Chicago Bulls, attempts to explain in his autobiography "Bad As I Wanna Be," why he prefers White women over Black women.

> *"When I was younger, I was not very attractive. Black girls didn't want to go out with me. I guess I still carry that resentment and that is why I prefer to be with White women."*

AS IF... White women were beating a path to his door when he was working as a janitor, with no hope of ever becoming successful. Before becoming famous, Dennis saw his African features and his powerful African physique as unattractive and worthless. It was a young Black girl who recognized his talent for playing basketball and took him to a local coach. It was also his two biological sisters, who were both All-American basketball players that helped him develop his game. Without the aid of plastic surgery, his self image changed once he discovered the gift that was hiding inside of him.

I do not believe that interracial or cross cultural relationships are wrong. Love certainly has the power to transcend race, color and creed. But we cannot use another human being as an escape hatch from self-hatred. We must accept and love ourselves for who we are apart from how we are viewed by others. If another human being has the power to make you feel beautiful and valuable, then that same person has the power to make you feel worthless.

I believe that Dennis Rodman suffers from the same malady that brought King Solomon to destruction. *"They both envied their oppressors."*

According to the Bible, King Solomon had more wealth and wisdom than any man that ever lived, but he clearly suffered from feelings of inferiority. For this reason he went and married an Egyptian princess as a status symbol.

The Egyptians oppressed the children of Israel for more than 400 years. Only through a series of miracles did God deliver Israel out of the hands of the Egyptians. King Solomon, above all people, knew the story of how Israel had suffered in Egypt, but because of the power and sophistication of the Egyptians, he ignored what they had done to his people. He saw the Egyptians as superior to the rag tag children of Israel. One of his crowning achievements, in his mind, was his marriage to an Egyptian princess. This was blatant disregard for Jewish law which stated that the children of Israel were not to marry outside of their own tribe. It was his relationships with women from other cultures, that Solomon believed to be superior, that led to his destruction.

There are Black men and women who turn to other races as a means of finding acceptance and validating their success. They don't want to be reminded of their African-American heritage. Nor do they want their children to carry "the stigma" of kinky hair and dark skin. They have no confidence in Black doctors, lawyers or other professionals. They feel more secure doing business with Whites because they have convinced themselves that "White is right!"

In many ways, Black women are just as guilty as Black men in perpetuating a false image of beauty. They continue in their futile attempts to escape from their heritage by moving to White neighborhoods, sending Black children to White schools, using lighter makeup, weaving their hair and/or having their nose and lips surgically altered.

I don't see anything wrong with adopting some of the positive attributes of other cultures, but it should never be used to make you feel better about yourself. Other cultures should feel privileged to know someone as talented and as awesome as you. You should see yourself as an ambassador to other cultures, introducing them to the *wonder-full* experience of being African-American. Our music, food, worship, and family life should generate pride and not shame.

* * *

Envy not your oppressor, and choose none of his ways. Proverbs 3:31

Climbing the Ladder of Self-Esteem

Kala's beautiful dark mahogany skin and chiseled features served as a perfect mask for her deep pain and feelings of inferiority. When she was a child her mother, who was an olive colored African American, married a White man. Thus began Kala's long and painful journey into a world of emotional, psychological and spiritual abuse. In public, her stepfather seemed to be kind and loving toward her, but behind closed doors, he brutalized her with words. He taunted her about her dark skin color and her short coarse hair. He said she looked more like a jungle animal than a human being. Whenever she got her hair washed, he laughed at her and referred to her hair as nappy and ugly. When he was angry, he would tell Kala that she was going to hell because she was too Black to go to heaven.

To make matters worse, Kala's mother soon gave birth to her half sister. They named her "Precious" because she was, in their eyes, so beauty-full. She had long curly hair and a light complexion and this met her stepfathers criteria for beauty.

Kala's first boyfriend was Hispanic with light skin and dark, wavy hair. After they moved in together, the pattern of abuse soon continued. He made fun of her, demoralized her, and on more than one occasion, she was beaten. She almost lost her life before she managed to escape from him.

When we first talked at a Bible study, Kala revealed that she was extremely depressed and frustrated. She had been on her job for eight years and was the only Black employee. Instead of making progress, her boss demoted her, cut her salary and insinuated that she was a thief.

Through it all, Kala thought it was her "Christian duty" to submit herself to her boss and to "turn the other cheek" so to speak. When we talked about her feelings, I could clearly see that after years of receiving nothing but negative information about herself, Kala had developed such a poor self-image, she felt abusive treatment was acceptable. In her mind, she was ugly and worthless. To make matters worse, she was very confused about how to respond to what was a clear cut case of abuse.

"Would it be right to let your dog sleep on your best dress so he can be comfortable?" I asked.

"Of course not!" she smiled.

"Then you must see yourself as too valuable to allow yourself to be mistreated. Just as God never intended for your dog to sleep on your best dress, He never intends for you to be misused or abused by anyone," I explained.

"But how can I tell my boss that he's treating me unfairly?" Kala said nervously. "I could get fired!"

It was easy to understand her anxiety. How could someone who thought that she was worthless challenge a powerful White man who was so much like her stepfather? It was my task to help her see herself as a beauty-full dress that was being used as a dog's blanket.

"It is your responsibility to recognize your value as a human being, and to set up boundaries for how you allow others to treat you," I began.

"If someone crosses the line that you have set for yourself, they must deal with the consequences of being confronted. It's up to you to find the courage to demand the respect that you are entitled to, or to remove yourself from an environment that is not beneficial to your physical, mental or emotional well-being."

Kala looked at me like I was speaking a foreign language. But the words began to sink in slowly. Perhaps you are waiting to hear that Kala quit her job or punched her boss. Life is not always that dramatic. However, the seeds of deliverance were planted as we prayed together across the table. The next time we talked, her posture was more erect. I could tell from just looking at her that the depression was lifting. She looked directly at me, not around me, or down at the ground. I could feel her smiling face saying, "I'm getting there."

As Kala continued to gain spiritual strength, she discovered the Word of God clearly tells us to confront the person who has offended us. It is important that we set "boundaries" for how we allow ourselves to be treated. For some people confrontation is harder than outrunning a freight train. But if fear sets in, encourage yourself through prayer and read Psalms 144, which tells us that the Lord will protect and deliver us from our enemies. Kala finally found the courage to face her boss. When we last talked, she was in the process of writing her union a letter, listing her grievances.

* * *

African-American women are in a constant struggle to climb the ladder of self-esteem without getting kicked off by people who feel they just don't belong at the top. The forces of darkness will use people and circumstances to keep you from fulfilling your purpose. No matter how successful you become, life will always present new challenges that will put your self-esteem to the test. Do I have the talent? Am I smart enough? Young enough? Thin enough? Will people accept me? Will I fail?

African American women come in all shapes, sizes and backgrounds. They may be found working in a factory, or in corporate America struggling to find acceptance, equal treatment, and equal wages. One coffee colored sister who is the executive V.P. of a major company still fumes about both White and Black visitors who come by her office, look her in the face and ask "Is your boss in?"

It happens to Black female physicians, lawyers, managers and consultants. "There is an element in our society that still doesn't know that the slaves have all been set free," a success-full Black business woman laughed. Without a doubt the attacks against women of color have taken their toll. I am constantly meeting Black women who may be extremely attractive on the outside, but *in the mirror of her mind, she sees herself as full of flaws.* She may be light skinned with long hair or she may be olive or ebony with short kinky hair. Either way, this lovely sister is haunted by feelings of being unattractive and undesirable. All too often she finds herself being misused by men because she is so desperate for acceptance and attention. She may wear a size ten dress and perceive herself as being grossly overweight. Many Black women don't realize that the bone density and muscle mass of African American women is different from Caucasian women. Because our bones and muscles are heavier by design, we can wear the same size dress as a White woman, yet weigh five to ten pounds more.

A woman with an identity crisis may try to disguise her feelings of inferiority by becoming an "overachiever." She views success and recognition as her ticket to acceptance by others. Her closet is full of designer clothing that will make her look and feel important. She drives an expensive car that everyone will identify with and still somewhere inside, a voice is telling her that she doesn't quite make the grade. This of course keeps her going in a circle chasing after another achievement that will only leave her feeling empty and alone.

Another sure sign of low self-esteem is the woman who is afraid to take risks. She lives her life in an invisible box that becomes her safety zone. She is afraid of changing jobs even if she hates being there. When opportunities for change come her way, she ignores them, makes excuses or doesn't even see the open door in front of her. She is afraid to confront a parent, husband, boyfriend, or boss, who is mistreating her, even when her life is threatened or she is on the brink of mental collapse.

She is afraid of trying because it may result in failure or rejection. Even something as simple as a new hair style or taking a special course of study is viewed as a tremendous risk. She is especially fearful of intimate relationships because of the possibility of being rejected or not measuring up to someone's expectations.

It is difficult to make a correct assessment of yourself without outside assistance. It is always easier to see another person's faults and short comings. But if you really want growth and positive change in your life, you should allow yourself to be carefully critiqued by a person who cares about you and wants you to become even more beauty-full than you are.

Sit down with a loving friend, a family member or a professional counselor and do a self assessment. Don't let the fear of what you might discover hinder you. Without a doubt you will find that for every weakness or shortcoming, you will have twice as many strengths and valuable attributes.

The following questions are designed to help you in your quest for self-discovery.

Spiritual Life:
1. Yes___ No___ Do you pray and read your bible and other related materials on a regular basis?

2. Yes___ No___ Do you attend church. Are you involved in outreach, choir, youth, etc.?

3. Yes___ No___ Are you involved in community activities that help the young, old, homeless people, etc.?

Gifts and Talents:

1. Yes___ No___ Have you taken the time to discover your gifts and talents?

2. Yes___ No___ Are you using your gifts effectively or in the process of perfecting your talents and gifts?

3. Yes___ No___ Are you willing to take the disappointments and criticisms that come with developing your special talents or gifts?

Personality:

1. Yes___ No___ Do your friends and family accuse you of being argumentative or having a bad attitude.

2. Yes___ No___ Are you shy or fearful when it comes to dealing with new or difficult situations.

3. Yes___ No___ Do you consider yourself patient and understanding when people are in trouble and need your help or advice?

Character:

1. Yes___ No___ Can you be trusted with sensitive and confidential information?

2. Yes___ No___ Are you open to criticism and correction, without getting upset?

3. Yes___ No___ Do you keep your word and your commitments once it has been given?

Take the time to discuss your answers to the above questions with a person who you believe will be honest and helpful. If they see you in a different light than you see yourself, please don't pout. Remember, honest words from a friend are better than flattery from an enemy.

The purpose of this exercise is to identify and blot out any and all traces of low-self esteem. Learning your strengths and weaknesses will help you develop high self-esteem and assist you in your quest to become more beauty-full.

Think of self-esteem as a success ladder that must be climbed. If you had a poor opinion of yourself, how you look, your personality, or talents and abilities, then hopefully this exercise will give you the courage to begin climbing the self-esteem ladder. Each rung of the ladder leads to a higher self-concept and better self image. Let's begin the exercise.

SELF ESTEEM LADDER

Spiritual discovery leads to self- discovery. When the inner man becomes spiritually strong, the outer man will find the strength to climb the ladder of self-esteem.

See Diagram On Page 40

THE TOP OF THE LADDER
Represents high self-esteem
This level of perception includes:
Wholeness - Self-acceptance -
Empowerment - Productivity - Positive Contributions

SEVENTH RUNG ON THE LADDER
Celebrate your life without sabotaging
your success.

SIXTH RUNG ON THE LADDER
Help others without becoming
fearful and intimidated.

FIFTH RUNG ON THE LADDER
Envision your self as success-full and
blessed.

FOURTH RUNG ON THE LADDER
Take pride in yourself, regardless
of your circumstances.

THIRD RUNG ON THE LADDER
Release the fears, hurts and
failures of the past.

SECOND RUNG OF THE LADDER
See through satanic traps of
self-hate and negativity.

FIRST RUNG OF THE LADDER
Believing you are valuable in the
sight of God.

THE BOTTOM OF THE LADDER
Represents low self-esteem.
This level of self perception includes:
Lack of confidence - Insecurity -
Procrastination - Destructive Behavior
Depression - Fear - Blame - Guilt - Suicide

Step one on the esteem ladder means to believe that God loves you and you are important and valuable to Him.

Whenever I meet people who see themselves as a worthless nobody, dumped in the trash-piles of life, I think of the story of the broken violin that was left in a junk shop. One day a master violinist came into the store. He picked up the old violin and made a few simple repairs. In spite of its scars and broken strings, the man saw that it was a very fine and rare instrument. Once he fixed it and began to play, others could see the real beauty and worth of the instrument. Many of us simply need the touch of the Master's hand for others to see how beauty-full and valuable we really are. God is the Master of fixing what is broken in your life and revealing the true gifts that are asleep within you.

Step two on the esteem ladder means to rise above all self-deception and negative traps set by the enemy.

It is hard to believe that so many people who see themselves as unattractive, undesirable and unacceptable were made to feel that way by people who claimed to love them. It is usually a family member who says or implies that a child is ugly because they have dark skin or short hair. A mother or father who withholds affection calls a child stupid or values one child over another.

For better or for worse, the opinion that you have of yourself is shaped by what others think of you. If you feel that you have failed to meet someone else's expectations or the standard of what they consider valuable, it is time to recognize that it is hatred and ignorance, and not truth that has shaped their distorted view. All too often a person who will not accept you, or makes you feel negative about yourself, has negative feelings about their own-selves. Have you ever been in a Funhouse or a House of Mirrors. Some of the trick mirrors are designed to make you look tall and skinny. Other mirrors are designed to make you look short and fat. We laugh at our reflection because we know the image that we are looking at is completely false. However, when the distorted mirror is found in a dysfunctional family, marriage, or by living in a racist society, it is no laughing matter. Negative words spoken during a time when our personalities are just being shaped can stay with us forever. Words like "you ain't never going to amount to nothing!," "stupid!," "ugly Black n_____." The scars left on our self-esteem can only be healed by words and actions that tell us that we are valuable. I thank God for the teachers who encouraged me as a child and for the older ladies in my church who told me that I was smart and a good little worker. They lovingly took my face in their hands and pronounced, "You're a sweet little thing."

It is up to you to let go of the lies that have been spoken against you as well as feelings of bitterness and unforgiveness. It is time to move on to all the blessings that God has for you.

Step three on the esteem ladder is to release the fears, hurts and failures of the past.

Nothing is more draining to a positive self-image than the memories that remind us of our past failures, heartaches and disappointments. We discover that we are handcuffed by fear when we even think about doing that which is productive and positive. Perhaps you need to be reminded of the trail of failures that litter the path of every successful person. Oprah Winfrey had a bad hair day and lost her job as a news anchor. She was given a small show on late night television. This led to her becoming the queen of the talk-show circuit. Jackie Joyner-Kersee lost at the Olympics only to return four years later to break three world records and win five Gold medals. Michael Jordan was cut from his High School basketball team. He went on to win four basketball championships. Sickness, divorce, heartache and failures are all a part of what shapes our

42

character and makes us stronger in the end. If you can't find anyone to encourage you... encourage yourself. If you can't find anyone to help you... help yourself. If no one will forgive you for your past mistakes... forgive yourself and forgive those people who let you down or hurt you. We all make mistakes in life. Just don't let the pain of the past, keep you from moving forward with your life.

The fourth step on the esteem ladder is to take pride in yourself regardless of your circumstances.

You may look at your circumstances and decide that you are a failure. Others may look at your life and tell you that you will never amount to anything. But most people who have become success-full in life can look back at a time when they were broke, uneducated, jobless, and even homeless. But with God's help the circumstances will eventually change. If you are at the bottom, you must see yourself as on the way to the top. If you feel as though your life is going nowhere, get off at the next exit and get some new directions. Once you get a new direction, you must have faith and confidence in the plan that God has for your life. Set new goals for yourself. Just working toward something positive will make you feel better about yourself. Get a High School diploma no matter what your age. Go back to college or a technical school, no matter what your circumstance. Read books or learn to read for your personal improvement. Select books on Black History. Read about great men and women of the Bible, biographies on Martin Luther King, Harriet Tubman and others. Create something with your own two hands like a special recipe or a handmade quilt. Write a book for your family that tell them all about you and your inner feelings. Any and all of these things will help you to rise above your circumstances.

Step five on the esteem ladder is to envision yourself as success-full and blessed.

The Bible says that without a vision, the people will perish. To have "vision" means the ability to see into the invisible realm. To "envision" is to have a picture inside of yourself of where you are going and what you will accomplish in life. Without self-esteem (which means to see yourself the way God sees you), you cannot see yourself as success-full and blessed. Your spiritual vision is blocked by fear and insecurity. But as you begin to accept the fact that you are power-full, gifted and entitled to the best that life has to offer, you can begin to experience God's blessings and live a success-full life.

The evidence of the unique blueprint of your design can be found in your own hands. Out of all the people on this earth, you have a set of fingerprints that are unlike anyone else's. You are truly one in a million. You can think thoughts, dream dreams, and create things that belong to you and you alone. Your potential is endless. The enemy is setting traps that are designed to keep you from being all that you were intended to be.

The vision you need comes from being close to or studying people who turned their vision into a reality. Madame C. J. Walker was the first Black female millionaire. She writes that she prayed and asked God to show her a way out of poverty. She also asked Him for a way to make her hair grow. In a dream, a man appeared to her and gave her the formula for her beauty products. She not only developed her hair products, but went from door to door selling her goods. Eventually, she built factories and operated Black beauty parlors all over the nation. Madame Walker had a vision and with hard work and God's help, it became a reality. Once you develop a strong spiritual life, you will become more sensitive to the things that cannot be seen with the natural eye. Prayer, fasting, and the

Word of God sharpen your spiritual insight. Soon you will begin to understand God's plan for your life. You will also see how to accomplish what God is calling you to do. This is called "vision." As God reveals your purpose and unique personality, you will envision yourself as successful and blessed.

The sixth step on the esteem ladder is to help others without becoming fearful and intimidated.

The most amazing discovery about climbing to the top of the esteem ladder is the discovery that the rungs of the ladder are made up of people and events that are used to help us climb up higher. All of these people are not loving and kind. All of the events are not pleasant. God especially uses the enemies who try to block us. In the end they become the stepping stones that allow us to climb up higher. He uses people to slam the door in our faces, only to force us to try the door that was really meant for us. We should never allow people or events in our past to keep us from being open and willing to help others. For every person who is against you, there will be two that are on your side. For every difficult circumstance, you will learn how to overcome.

The most important testimony of your wholeness will come from the people who have been personally inspired and helped by you. I heard a person say that emulation is the best evidence of your greatness. Don't be angry when someone tries to find out the secrets of your success. Take it for what it is... a compliment. Please don't buy the lies that if you teach someone or mentor someone, they will one day take your position. You shouldn't be planning to stay in that position. You should be looking forward to moving up higher and training someone to replace you.

If your goal is to make this world a better place, then see your sister as a partner and co-laborer. We live on a planet that needs as much help as it can get. Be a mentor and encourager. As you open doors for others, doors will be opened for you.

The seventh step on the esteem ladder is to celebrate your life without sabotaging your success.

I have known countless people who worked long and hard to reach a desired goal only to deliberately and willfully push the self-destruct button. There are several reasons why a person who seems to have it all together will suddenly self-destruct. The downhill spiral may begin with a false concept of what it really means to be success-full. Career success does not guarantee success in your personal relationships. A busy schedule can be a liability instead of an asset. The fantasy of "no more hard work... I can finally relax and enjoy my life," is a fantasy indeed. In reality, success creates greater physical, emotional and mental challenges. If a person is unprepared for the grueling demands of being at the top, they will eventually find a way to bail out.

Another reason for reaching the top of the ladder only to tumble back down again is the residue of feelings of guilt and/or low self-esteem. No matter how high you climb, you may experience a nagging voice of negativity that keeps saying you don't deserve to live a productive and success-full life. "You're not good enough... if people knew the real you, they wouldn't think you were so great."

Those negative thoughts must not be buried, but confronted with truth. Nobody is perfect... and no matter how hard we try, we will never have it all together. We become success-full in spite of our limitations and disabilities. I could tell myself I am such a poor speller, that I should never think of writing one sentence, let alone a whole book. Instead of giving in to the voice of negativity, I have learned to confront it by saying, "My task is to keep writing no matter what!!" Someone will come along who is a great speller and will be glad to help me reach my goal.

You must decide in advance that you will go the distance. Be prepared to work hard but at the same time, make sure your life is balanced and productive. When the temptation to push the self-destruct button comes, ask God to give you the inner strength to hold on to your blessings.

I have a beauty-full play daughter named Brita. I am twenty years her senior and I can truly say that being around her keeps me feeling young. Brita is tall and pleasingly plumb. For some people, this may be viewed as a problem, but not Brita. She is too busy celebrating her life. Brita is the kind of person who sings out in the middle of a busy street or strikes up a conversation with a perfect stranger. For Brita, there are no strangers, only people she doesn't know very well. Once, not long ago, when I was a committed workaholic, it was Brita who encouraged me to learn how to celebrate life. I was working very late one night when Brita dropped by my office. She was not impressed at all with my hard work and dedication.

"When you die, I'm gonna cash your insurance policy in and have a good time," Brita laughed. On that note, I decided that I needed to stop taking myself so seriously and learn how to have fun. Once you become success-full, and you will, be sure that you take time to enjoy yourself. It's good to have things as long as those things don't have you.

* * *

The "Brick House" Syndrome

Have you ever wondered why men are so fixated on big breasts and wide hips? Why not slender hips and small breasts? What makes one more sensuous than the other?

How many times have you watched a man, watch a woman? He stops at a red light and immediately his eyes are drawn to a woman crossing the street. As she walks in front of his car, he studies her carefully. First, he looks at her face, then her hair. His eyes move down to her breasts. As she passes by the car and steps onto the sidewalk, he studies her waist, buttocks and legs. If she meets his criteria for "fine," he smiles or maybe makes a statement:

"Wooowee... baby got back!" he proclaims. A simple translation would be, the woman looks good and has a big butt.

But have you ever wondered why the appearance of the face and the shape of a woman is so important to men?

We learn from psychologists that humans memorize the faces of other humans for the purpose of identification. We can look through a crowd and pick out the person we are searching for by recognizing their facial features.

The face also communicates thoughts and feelings. When we are interacting with another human, we smile or frown, stare or look away. In a hundred different ways, our facial expressions convey what words may not tell us. We can also tell about a person's physical and mental health from their eyes, nose, lips and teeth.

It is part of our genetic makeup (things we do out of instinct) to protect ourselves and reproduce "after our own kind." Every creature that was ever created has a strong desire to live and to reproduce itself. This is how God created life. In the book of Genesis, He commanded every living thing to multiply after its own kind. As much as we hate roaches and rats, if you try to kill one of them, they will run for their lives. The lowest form of life will do everything possible to hold on to life and reproduce more of their kind.

If a roach knows that it's life is valuable, and does everything in it's power to protect itself, then why would someone made in the image of God try to throw their life away?

Genetic coding causes the male to look for the best of the female species for the purpose of reproducing strong and healthy children. Prehistoric men were concerned about the shape of a woman's body because it was directly related to the preservation of their offspring. It was believed that a woman with full breasts could feed more than one child during periods where food might be hard to come by. The breast are also man's first experience at being nurtured, comforted and fed. This early birth experience causes him to always be drawn to the breast of a woman.

Because primitive people were for the most part nomadic, meaning they moved around a lot, men found that women with wide hips and full buttocks had fewer miscarriages. Strong and shapely legs and feet meant that they could recover from childbirth more quickly and continue to travel with other members of the tribe.

Over the centuries, men have lost the motive behind their attraction to big breasts and wide hips. Because of progress and changing life-styles, the survival of the tribe has been reduced to employment vs. unemployment. Women no longer have to be strong and well endowed to have children, but the male instincts are the same. "Sexy," still translates to big breasts and wide hips.

The concept of facial attractiveness is also deeply rooted in our heritage. The face helps to determine the person's tribal identity. The onlooker derives a sense of what the persons cultural and social preferences might be as he studies the color, texture and bone structure of the face and hair. If the skin is dark, the nostril wide and the lips full, the person making the assessment will feel a connection if he or she is of the same persuasion. But if the lips are thin and the complexion pale, then there is a chance that the person may find the object of their focus less attractive.

This is because in ancient times, the member of a different tribe or racial group might be a part of a hostile or warring faction. To a great degree, this concept is still practiced in our society today. Whites war against Blacks; Jews against Arabs; Crips against Bloods; etc. But humans of all tribes and races are more than animals attempting to survive and reproduce after their own kind. We as humans have something that animals do not have. We have souls. It is the inner-man who has needs that go beyond survival.

We need more than physical attraction. We search for our "soul-mate," the person who not only looks healthy and attractive, but one who is spiritually and intellectually compatible. This search causes us to look beyond the surface of another human being and into the beauty of their very heart and soul.

* * *

Outer
Scars–Inner Beauty

While some of the issues that rob us of our self-esteem are clearly based on a distorted value system, other issues can represent real challenges to women of all backgrounds:

•Surgical procedures that disfigure or remove a breast, uterus, or other body parts.

•Diseases that cause the loss of hair, loss of weight, or scarring, like Cancer and AIDS.

•A pregnancy that bloats and distorts the figure.

•Aging that causes balding, graying, wrinkles, and change in body shape.

•Birth defects or accidents resulting in deafness, blindness, or crippling.

•Gland dysfunctions, eating disorders, or medications that cause extreme weight gain.

Women who have been robbed of their sense of beauty

live in a world of isolation. They see and appreciate others, but they believe that they are either terrible to look at, or no one really sees them or cares about their presence or existence.

The beautiful woman next to you, behind you, or in front of you can be clearly seen. But you are always over-looked, like you don't really exist. You are in another dimension. It's almost like you are from another world, the planet of Rejected People.

Let me remind you again, that only 10% of our beauty is visible to the eye. 90% of our real beauty is on the inside.

I am thankful that there are still people in the world who dare to cross the boundaries of another person's pain and isolation. There are people who can see beneath the surface of a less than perfect exterior and find the hidden treasure that God has placed within. *Personality* - can transcend deformity. *Spirit* - runs much deeper than scars that disfigure. *Character* - can triumph over racial bigotry. *Talent* - will open more doors than looks or gender.

It is only through the eyes of the spirit that we can perceive the true beauty of another human being. We must learn to rely on our inner-vision in order to see the *beauty-in-full*. The exterior is just a small part of what constitutes beauty.

* * *

"God Turned My Wounds Into Weapons" would be a perfect title for Linda's story.

"I first heard you speak in Miami. It was 1990," Linda smiled at me from across the table.

"You said that God was the only one who could turn

our 'wounds into weapons.' Those words helped me get through an ordeal that changed my life forever."

I stared at the lovely young woman, curious to hear her story. She smiled revealing a set of perfect white teeth. Her brown eyes and delicate features gave no clue to the suffering that she had endured for the past six years.

It happened late one afternoon as Linda and two young exchange students were returning from work. A Bronco truck attempted to pass her. As she made a right turn the truck hit her car at full speed. One of the students riding with her was killed instantly. Linda, who was only twenty eight at the time, remained in a coma clinging to life for more than a month. She awoke suffering from memory loss. Both of her shoulders were broken. Her pelvic bone was also broken in three places. Her legs were broken, and to make matters worse, the inside metal door handle was lodged in her right thigh. Broken glass was embedded under her skin, scaring her upper body.

After being hospitalized for three months, the nightmare was just beginning. Gangrene developed in her right thigh. For three years the wound in her leg had to remain open to allow for drainage and the regeneration of new tissue. On top of everything else she was arrested and tried for manslaughter. The medication caused her to gain more than ninety pounds. And through it all, there was the battle with pain and narcotics.

"All my life I hated my big thighs," Linda laughed. "But now I know that everything about the way I was formed was a part of a bigger plan."

"You see, it was the fat and thick muscle tissue in my upper legs that kept the door handle from shattering my thigh bone. They would have had to amputate my leg if it had not been for my 'fat thighs'!"

"When the accident first happened, all I could think about was living the rest of my life with scars and deformities. But as time passed, my attitude changed drastically." Linda had a glow about her as she continued.

"Something happened on the inside of me that made me see life differently. I learned how to appreciate simple things. I stopped being concerned about how my body looked, I just wanted to walk again. As my suffering continued, I learned about humility, perseverance, and determination. I learned how to suffer without complaining. I learned to believe in things that doctors said could never happen. I discovered the woman of faith and power that was living inside of me. Because of what I went through, I know who I really am."

Linda's story is a clear picture of how a "deep" experience revealed the treasure that was buried inside of her.

Many times it isn't until we are in "deep water" that we discover our true character and nature. It is the "deep waters" of life that reveal our real gifts and purpose.

In the writings of Isaiah, Jesus Christ was also described as one who suffered and was despised by men. If there is anyone who understands the pain of rejection, He who was betrayed and crucified, surely does. As he hung on the cross, he made an amazing statement: "Father forgive them for they know not what they do."

Unfortunately, there were those who could not see into the heart of one who was so full-of-beauty and so full-of-love that he was willing to lay down his life for others. Jesus could have become bitter because he was rejected. Bitterness is a strong substance that eats away at the inner-beauty.

Instead of becoming bitter, he remained focused on the mission that his Father had sent him to accomplish. His work was to save the lost, heal the sick and set the captives free. He never let what people thought of him keep him from accomplishing his goals. Just because you have a disability, or there is something about yourself that makes you feel unattractive, remember that your body is not the "whole you."

Let your good works and beautiful spirit transcend your physical appearance until the beauty-full woman that God created you to be shines like the brightest star in heaven.

* * *

Those who do business in great waters, see the miracles that God performs in the deep. Psalms 107:23-24

Perfect for God's Purpose

How many times have you asked yourself, *"If I was truly created by God and made in His image, why couldn't He have done a better job? Why does someone else seem to have all the talent and all the good looks? Why does it seem like God favors some people more than others? If God is loving, kind and compassionate, why does He allow people to be born with obvious flaws, birth defects or disabilities? Are they being punished? Did God make a mistake?"*

When my youngest daughter Theresa was six years old, I was faced with finding the answer to the most difficult question that I have ever been asked. She was born with three fingers on each hand. Her right leg was three inches shorter than her left leg. This did not stop her from playing the piano and the harp. One night after saying her prayers, she asked a profound question. "Mommie," she began, "if God loves me, then why did my daddy die and why was I born this way?"

The question shook me to the core because I had laid awake many nights asking God the same question, but I'm not sure I expected an answer. Now things were different. I had to find an answer for my precious little girl that would satisfy her mind and at the same time, help her to maintain a positive and loving view of God.

I cleared my throat and tried to answer.

"I don't know why you were born with missing fingers and a short leg... but I promise that I will ask God to give me an answer."

That night I fell on my knees weeping and asked the Lord to give me the answers I so desperately needed. As I sat on the floor in the darkness of my room the Lord spoke to my heart. His words were few, but powerful and unforgettable. He simply said: *"Tell Theresa that she is perfect for my purpose."*

I cannot understand to this very day how those words seemed to satisfy and quiet her heart, but she nodded her head as if she understood perfectly, because somewhere inside of her she did understand more perfectly than I could ever imagine.

Theresa grew up facing the stares, whispers and taunts of her peers. Somehow she got through it and went away to college. While living in Washington D.C., she became an intern for the National Right To Life, the premier organization for the "Pro-Life movement."

One weekend she called home. Her voice was full of excitement. "Mom, remember when God told you that I was perfect for His purpose? Well, He was right!" she said. "I just came back from a meeting with a Pro-Choice group. They tried to argue the point that a woman who has prior knowledge that her fetus is deformed should have a right to abort. They tried to say that the child would be better off if it were never born. At that moment I knew that I was the perfect person for the debate. I went to the microphone and held up my three fingers," she continued.

"I told the Pro-Choice people, face to face, how my life had been meaningful and highly productive in spite of the way I was born. I had a chance to say that the circumstances of our birth has nothing to do with my destiny."

I was blown away as I hung up the telephone. Now I could see the power that God has unleashed in my daughter. I listen as she encourages young people who feel that they have no value or purpose. She sat next to a young woman who was blind with failing kidneys. Theresa was able to encourage her and give her a sense of hope and purpose. Because of her experiences, she is able to help confused and rejected women gain a new sense of "I-am-some-body-ness."

He never promised us a rose garden, but He did promise us the victory. He did say that we were more than conquerors. He did say that He would cause us to always triumph.

Most of what we believe about ourselves are distortions of the truth. These distortions come because we see ourselves through the eyes of the enemy and not the eyes of the One who loves us and created us for His purpose. The real enemy at work behind racial bigotry and Hollywood typecasting is Satan himself. He works on our minds, as well as the minds of others creating false images and standards that are popularized by the media.

If you believe that you are ugly, worthless, stupid, or that your race, gender, age, or appearance makes you unacceptable, then you will believe that the God who made you is not perfect because, after all, you were God's big mistake.

It is important to note that it was the preoccupation with superficial beauty that led to Satan's downfall. If Lucifer (Satan's name before the fall) had worked to maintain his character and integrity in the sight of God instead of becoming obsessed with his appearance, popularity and power, he would not have become an outcast.

On the other side of the coin of being unattractive are the people who, in the physical sense, are very attractive. Unfortunately, many people who are physically attractive learn to depend on their looks to gain advantages in life. But as time goes by, we all must learn the sometimes painful lesson: *Physi-*

cal appearance is like a summer rose, splendid while in bloom, but fading much too soon.

If a person's life has been centered around their external attributes, there is a good chance that they may never discover the beauty within.

> *We must be careful not to allow our outward appearance to make us less committed to the development of our inner gifts and talents.*

A pretty face can be a curse rather than a blessing if it hinders a woman from discovering the beauty within. Physical attractiveness can become the cloak that hides a multitude of insecurities, hurts and fears. A young girl or woman who seeks attention by always having her body on display is a classic example of:

•Believing that her "sexy" appearance will give her the advantage that she would not have if she were less revealing.

•Believing that she has nothing more to offer than her body, so she uses it to get the attention she so desperately needs.

•She was never taught that her body is so beauty-full and valuable, that she should protect it at all costs. Like money or precious jewels that are kept in a safe place, her valuable body should be kept out of the reach of thieves and abusers.

The woman who does not understand how to manage her outer beauty, can easily fall into a cycle of being misused and abused. Even though there is a deterioration in the moral values of our society, a wise woman will not fall prey to a life-style that is designed to degrade and disrespect her. Like fine china, that which is valuable should be cherished and handled with respect and consideration.

You don't have to have a baby to prove your love for a man. You don't have to "shack-up" because a man doesn't love you enough to marry you. And you certainly don't have to borrow another woman's husband because you don't believe that you could ever have a man of your own.

It is very possible that childhood abuse may also be at the core of a woman's confused and/or destructive behavior. Abuse, whether it is sexual, physical or verbal can leave deep spiritual scars. People who are damaged on the inside suffer just as much as people with outer scars and disabilities. Fear and bitterness can rob us of a beautiful smiling face; a broken spirit makes the outer body seem weak and unattractive.

Once a woman's looks begin to fade, (and they will fade more rapidly if she is being abused) it may be too late to develop her inner beauty and talents. This happens because a woman with fading beauty is usually the last one to realize that she is no longer young and attractive.

It was this same false perception of beauty that led to Satan's destruction. Whenever the lure of outward appearance is used to promote a selfish agenda, it will ultimately lead to self-destruction, as well as the pain and destruction of those who are caught in the web of seduction.

* * *

Wounded Butterflies

The beauty that emanates from a woman is in many ways like that of a splendid butterfly. I once heard a poet describe a butterfly as a flower with wings.

Because of it's beauty and fragile structure, this magnificent specimen of God's handywork must face many challenges. First, it is difficult for the butterfly to camouflage its beauty. At times, it will hide in the petals of a flower in full bloom, but once it takes flight with all of it's brilliant colors and delicate wing structure, it is in full view of potential predators like birds, lizards, spiders and other powerful insects. Unfortunately, the butterfly has no built in defense mechanisms. It cannot fly with great speed and it has great difficulty finding a place to hide. Its protection and survival is clearly in the hands of God.

All too often women are faced with this same dilemma. They try to face the world with their fears and doubts carefully tucked away beneath their beauty-full wings, but the predators are always lurking and they are very real and very deadly.

Many women discover too late that the man who they thought would be their protector was in fact a predator in disguise. It may happen as suddenly as a woman going out on a date, only to end up as the victim of a vicious rape, or she might find herself being stalked by an ex-boyfriend or husband who refuses to let her go. Any woman who has gone through a painful experience can tell you that the emotional and psychological scarring can last a lifetime.

Other women may find themselves in a long term relationship that is a living hell.

It feels like I'm nothing," Connie, a precious African sister, cried as I held her in my arms. "I hate him for what he did to me."

Connie's story would make anyone's blood boil. "He would drag me out of my bed and beat me and kick me in front of my children. Then he would tell them terrible lies about me. He would tell them that I was a stupid, worthless, tramp and was getting what I deserved. I could have taken the beatings... but not in front of my children," she sobbed.

Domestic violence is one of the most destructive forces that has ever plagued women. Not only does it have the potential to take a woman's life, but it destroys her self-esteem and her will and desire to express her talents and gifts. It destroys her confidence and her ability to think independent thoughts. It destroys her humanity, along with the beauty of her soul and spirit.

I have counseled women who feel so worthless that they are willing to sell their bodies on the street or participate in other kinds of illegal and degrading activity to please their abusers. The prisons are full of decent, yet misguided women who have fallen into the trap of mental and emotional abusers.

The reward for those who have tried to defend themselves against their predators can be seen in the faces of the women I have ministered to all over the country. Their lives become a maze of broken bones and scarred faces. These women will develop mental problems, become suicidal, and all too often die prematurely.

Other women live in prisons of self-hatred or self-deception. They may be the wife, or girlfriend of a man who appears to be friendly and is very successful. He may be a preacher, politician or hold a good job. In one highly publicized case of abuse, the woman's husband was the Chief of Police in a small bedroom community.

Self-hatred makes a woman believe that it is her laziness, stupidity and disobedience that drives her man to abuse her. Many divorced women believe that no matter how terrible her partner behaved, she is somehow responsible for the breakup of the marriage. It is even more painful when he finds a new partner, and rebuilds his life, leaving her guilt ridden, bitter and out in the cold with children to raise. In spite of all the high profile divorce cases where women walk away with millions of dollars, in reality, countless women have come away from courtrooms and lawyers' offices with no compensation or support for herself or her children, and frequently no knowledge of his whereabouts.

To make matters worse, she and her children must face the pain of being rejected and the feeling that they were not worthy of love and affection.

The newly separated or divorced woman finds that a turbulent relationship can be easier to bare than no relationship at all. This is why even after the humiliation of divorce, the withdrawal can be so painful that women continue to allow their ex-husbands' sexual privileges in exchange for the financial and emotional support she needs.

Women trapped in deception keep hoping that he will change or that things will get better. They may at some point discover that she is worse off than the woman who has been through a divorce. She believes that she is enduring the pain to keep her family together. In her delusion she blames herself, the children, financial pressures, his job, or his unemployment for his abusive behavior. Other women are bound by fear that runs so deep, they refuse to seek help or counseling of any kind. A pastor's wife who was being abused was told that it was God's will for her to stay with her husband. **Let me say in bold type that there is no place in the Bible where a woman is to remain under the same roof with a man who is a threat to her life, the lives of her children, or her sanity.** If anyone tries to tell you to stay with an abuser, let them take your place for a few days while you look for a safe place to rebuild your life. **1-800-799-SAFE(7233)** is the 24 hour hotline for the center for National Domestic Violence. It offers assistance for women or children who are being abused. Those who know of someone who is being abused and would like to know how to help, can also use this number.

Statistics show that 50% of all murdered females are killed by their husbands or boyfriends. 63% of young men ages 11-20 who are in prison for murder, killed their mother's abuser.

Many women fear that if they manage to escape from their abusers, they will face a life of poverty, unemployment and loneliness.

In their minds they are like caterpillars: ugly, despised, creeping things that are getting what they deserve. But in the eyes of God, they are one step away from being transformed into beauty-full butterflies.

Many years ago, a dear friend called me early one morning. After a severe beating, she finally realized that one more day with her husband might cost her life. Fortunately, he had no idea where I lived, or that his wife might be hiding at my house. She was so badly beaten that it was weeks before she recovered. Late one night, I took her to the airport where she caught a plane that would take her to live with a family member in another city. Today, she is a poised, confident, success-full businesswoman. Whenever I see her, I can hardly believe that she is the same woman who was so timid and fearful that she almost lost her life.

If you are in a life threatening situation, don't try to think about where you will live or how you will make it. Once you step out in faith, doors will open for you and your children. God has worked miracles for thousands of women and I know He can and will make a way for you and your children to survive.

As awful as it is for a woman to live with physical abuse, mental abuse can be just as painful. The pain is felt in your mind and spirit instead of your body. Men who lie, cheat, disrespect and abandon women are simply using a different kind of weapon to wound and destroy them. The horror stories range from women who have caught their husbands in bed with other men, to women who lost their husband to a close friend.

Men who have molested their children, destroyed the family financially, deserted their wives for a younger woman, or gotten themselves strung out on drugs or alcohol leave behind tremendous suffering. If a six on the Richter scale is considered a big jolt, then classify these woman as experiencing a ten. Their lives are in shambles and it feels like their chances of rebuilding are slim to none. There is a special blessing for people who come to the aid of women and children who have been both abused and abandoned.

The more subtle type of abuse is called *"control."* A "controller" does not allow a woman to manage her money or her life, even when she works everyday. She has no control over the decisions and is made to feel confused or stupid about the choices she makes when she tries to act independently from the man, parent, or friend who controls her. She does not have the freedom to come and go as she pleases and must account for her relationships with people and her whereabouts at all times. Even church attendance and giving tithes and offerings can become a point of contention in her relationship. A controller is a manipulator and may even use religious teachings to make his wife or girlfriend submit to his desires. This woman lives like a caged bird. Even if the door is left open, her wings have been psychologically clipped. In her mind she has lost her ability to fly.

At work she is the expert. At home she is stupid. At church she is a leader. At home she makes wrong decisions. At social gatherings she is attractive and funny. At home she is overweight and boring. At her children's school, she is praised. At home she's not a good mother. Her future will take her in one of three directions. (1) She will eventually become one of the "living dead..." doing what she is told and losing all sense of her personal identity. (2) She will rebel and do something that is both crazy and unproductive, like have an affair, use drugs or alcohol, gain a hundred pounds, starve herself to death, or commit suicide. (3) She will wake up and discover who she is and ask God to help her in the fight to take control of her life.

All of the wounds that have been inflicted on women are not necessarily from relationships with men. Many women grow up in abusive homes. Mothers have destroyed their daughters. Fathers have left emotional scars that may never heal. Teachers, relatives and the neighbor next door could easily be a predator in disguise. Whether you were raped, molested, beaten, abandoned, or raised by alcoholics and drug addicts, the issue is not who inflicted the wound, but how do you find healing.

I urge you not to bury your pain, but to deal with it so that you can become a whole, functional and beauty-full woman. Failure to deal with hurt and anger will rob you of your beauty and destroy your life in many different ways.

1. A woman who is angry instantly loses her beauty. It distorts her face and ruins her gentle body language. Nobody wants to be around a

woman whose body is tight and her words bite. The 'hand on the hip,' 'neck rollin' Black woman is an image that we should fight to rid ourselves of at all cost.

2. A woman who is bitter, jealous and envious can be a living nightmare. Her face sends a message that trouble is imminent. The environment becomes tense and uneasy when she is around because no one knows if a simple statement will cause an explosion or will be used against them at a later time.

3. A woman who is hurting instantly ages, no matter how young she is, she seems old and weary. Her conversation is negative and there is no joy when she is around. This woman is also a good candidate for alcohol and drug addiction. Many of the drug addicted women that I have counseled got hooked in an attempt to free themselves from the pain of just being alive.

Many of us are bearing the scars of living with a family member who is addicted to drugs or alcohol. Or maybe, to bring it closer to home, you are currently a victim of drug or alcohol addiction. If you have lost your job, your marriage, your children and your dignity, then I rejoice with you. Why? Because you have nothing left to lose and nowhere to go but up!

While I am a firm believer in professional counseling, it is still the "Wonder-full Counselor," who brings about deep inner-healing. Your Heavenly Father sees the child in you that is afraid to face the memories and the monsters of the past. He sees the weak and broken woman who thinks that she doesn't have the strength to break free from addiction. In 2 Corinthians 12:9 the Lord says: "My power shows up best in weak people." He is a strong tower, the Comforter and the Protector who will take you by the hand and give you the courage to face your fears.

Find a quiet place and read Psalm 27:1: The Lord is my light and my salvation. Why then should I be afraid? When evil men come to destroy me they will stumble and fall. The Lord is the strength of my life; there is nothing for me to fear.

When God is present in your life, nothing can hurt you and nothing can keep you in bondage. Tell Him about your failures and your fears. Go back to the beginning, laying every painful experience at His feet. If you know you were abused, but you can't remember the details, pray and ask God to show you what really happened. It may be difficult to get it out, but once you do it, you will find that the pain and fear will begin to diminish. Next comes the hard part, but you can do all things through Christ who strengthens you. You must see your abusers for who they really are... full of fear, confusion, pain and in desperate need of God's deliverance. Pray for them asking God to set them free from the demonic stronghold that controls them. If they are deceased or whereabouts unknown, ask God to break the spirit of fear and hatred that you hold in your heart against them.

Forgiving the one who hurt you is the only way that you can be truly free. Please understand that forgiveness is not only words that are spoken, but forgiveness is a long and sometimes difficult process where you must release the memory of what was done to you. Each time you rehearse painful events, you produce a substance in your spirit that is called bitterness.

Bitterness creates a number of problems. It keeps you from having happy, loving, relationships. It keeps you addicted to something that will not take away your pain. It keeps you from moving forward in life because you are trapped in the

memories of the past. The misery inside of you will contami-
nate the people around you and create sickness in your spirit
that will manifest in the form of migraine headaches, ulcers,
high blood pressure and even cancer.

Forgiveness means that when the memories come, you
must make a conscious decision not to be angry with the person. You must refuse to allow the past to be played over and
over again in your mind. Ask God to erase the tapes of the past
and replace it with a plan for the future. The right professional counselor can help you find deliverance from past hurts.
However you do it, don't be enslaved by the monster of abuse.
Do everything in your power to break free. It's time to break
out of your dark cocoon and spread your beauty-full wings
and fly.

* * *

God wants to "Father" You

Do you ever have questions about your beauty and value? Do you ever wonder why certain things have happened in your life? If so, you are entitled to an answer directly from the one who designed you and breathed the breath of life into you.

God is more than the Creator of all mankind. He is also *"FATHER"* to all those who will acknowledge Him and desire to become His children. That is why the Lord said in 2nd Corinthians: *"Leave the ungodly; separate yourselves from them; don't touch their filthy things, and I will welcome you, and be a Father to you, and you will be my sons and daughters."*

Many of us have heard or recited what is sometimes called The Lord's Prayer. It begins with *"Our Father, who art in heaven..."* The opening sentence tells us that the Father whom we are praying to is not a biological father made of flesh. God is a spirit. He is not Black, White, or any other culture. The prayer is addressed to our spiritual Father who is in heaven. Although we have never seen Him face to face, through the Bible we learn about His personality, His character and His love for His children.

The challenge for many of us who have accepted God

as our Heavenly Father is that our thoughts, feelings and images of our earthly father sometimes can and will influence our relationship with our Heavenly Father.

Answer the following questions about your relationship with your earthly father:

•Did you grow up without a father?
•Did your father disown you or claim you were not his child?
•Did your father abuse you with words?
•Did your father tell you that you were stupid or ugly?
•Did your father abuse you sexually, or physically threaten or beat you?
•Was your father unable or unwilling to provide for you?
•Was your father always breaking his promises?
•Was your father very strict and mean?
•Was your father weak or addicted to drugs or alcohol?
•Did your father fail to show you love or affection?

Any of these negative perceptions of your natural father will cause you to have a distorted view of your Heavenly Father. If your earthly father did not love you and value you, then why would your Heavenly Father treat you any different?

If you believe you were created in the image of your Heavenly Father, and you see him in the image of your earthly father, then you may have difficulty trusting your Heavenly Father to meet your needs. You may have trouble believing that your Heavenly Father will protect you and provide for you.

Last but not least, if your earthly father never told you that he loves you and sees you as uniquely beautiful and special, then how can the reality of your Heavenly Father's love find its way into your heart?

It will be difficult to see your Heavenly Father as good, kind, intelligent, and power-full if your biological father is just the opposite. And if you are his child, the child of a weak, bad tempered failure, then how can you be any better?

If you have experienced a painful relationship at the hands of your natural father that has damaged your self image, then *it is important to understand what your Heavenly Father has done to save you, restore you, and heal you from all of your hurts.*

As head of the Children's ministry at my church, I often come in contact with the most beautiful children who live with foster or adoptive parents. They were taken out of an abusive and/or dysfunctional family to protect them and give them a better life. In the beginning the children look frightened and lonely. They have to make new friends and learn new rules. But as they continue in an atmosphere of love and concern, they soon become happy and secure. Love has the power to heal the deepest hurts, and God is love!

Reading the book of Romans, I discovered that our Heavenly Father made the same provision for us as children who may have been rejected or abused. *Romans 8:15-16: (Living) But you are no longer in bondage to fear, for you have been adopted into the family of God, and now you may cry out to Him, "Father, Father." For the Holy Spirit will speak to our hearts and let us know for sure that we are really the children of our Heavenly Father.*

Your Heavenly Father wants you to have the following assurance:

•You are His child and not a stepchild.
•After you confess your sins you are completely forgiven for everything.

•He hears your prayers and delights in blessing you!
•He has a special plan for your life that he will reveal to you.
•He will give you the desires of your heart.
•You are beautiful and special to him.
•He will always provide for you.
•He will always protect you.
•He will never hurt you or abuse you.
•He will never condemn you, criticize you or judge you unfairly.

Becoming a child of God begins with accepting Jesus Christ as Lord and Savior of your life. Jesus is the only doorway to your Heavenly Father. *Your "new birth" means that you now take on the attributes of your Heavenly Father.* You no longer have to deal with *"birth defects,"* because you are *"Born Again."*

You don't have to say: *"I was born poor..." "I was born with a bad temper..." "I was born with a learning disability..."* As the *"new you"* begins to develop, you will find healing, wholeness and miraculous changes taking place in your life.

My goddaughter was a very pretty little girl on the outside, but she was born with a disability called dyslexia. Her eyes saw words backwards, therefore she couldn't learn to read. After she gave her heart to the Lord, she became a new creation. Within one year the dyslexia disappeared. She was able to go to a regular school and later graduate.

God loves to work miracles in the lives of His children. You may be saying to yourself that your situation is beyond God's help, but here's the good news, God delights in the tough cases and with Him nothing is too hard and nothing is impossible.

Here's a scripture to paste on your bathroom mirror:

Jeremiah 32:27: "Behold, I am the Lord, the God of all flesh. Is there anything too hard for Me?"

But what do we know about Father God? What are his attributes and how will we become like Him?

•We know that He is a **scientist** because he created the universe.
•We know He is an **artist** because of the beauty of the universe.
•We know He is a **writer** because He has given us His Word.
•We know He is a **doctor** because He healed the sick.
•We know He is a **psychologist** because He has given us peace of mind.
•We know He is a **parent** because He calls us His children.
•We know that He is a **teacher** because He has given us his wisdom.
•We know that He is **loving** because God is love.
•We know that He is **wealthy** because the earth is the Lord's.
•We know that He is **generous** because He will supply our needs.
•We know that He is **merciful** because His mercy endures forever.

These are only a few of God's attributes. Remember, we are God's children. All that is in God, is potentially in us. We must simply learn how to unlock our potential.

Try the following step to help you reach your full potential:

YOU MUST BE "BORN AGAIN:" The process is simple. In a church with a Christian friend, or even in a quiet place by yourself, say this simple prayer: "Lord Jesus, I know that the Father sent you so that I can experience a better life and eternal life. I ask you now to come into my heart and make me a new creation. I ask you to forgive my sins and show me how to live a life that is pleasing to you. Amen."

YOU MUST GROW SPIRITUALLY: Build relationships with people who can help you grow into your full potential. Find a church that teaches the whole Bible. You cannot be fully changed without developing spiritually. Attend worship services and Bible studies on a regular basis. Get involved in a ministry or community service where you can serve others and not focus on yourself so much. As you get involved in serving, your special gifts and talents will begin to surface.

YOU MUST BE TRANSFORMED: Ask God to show you and help you in the areas of your life where change is needed. Try not to resist when your Father allows events to come that are designed to bring about transformation. Be willing to make the sacrifices that are necessary to develop your gifts and talents. This may mean going back to school or changing your friends, job, profession or life-style.

AFFIRM YOURSELF DAILY: The word of God has hundreds of affirmations that speak of your Father's love for you and remind you how awesome you are.

- *Romans 8:37* - I am more than a conqueror.
- *Psalms 139:14* - I am fearfully and wonderfully made.
- *Song of Solomon 4:7* - I am beautiful and there is no spot in me.
- *Psalm 1:3* - I shall be like a tree bringing forth fruit in my season.

•*Philippians 4:13* - I can do all things through Christ who strengthens me.

•*Ephesians 2:10* - I am His workmanship, created in Christ Jesus for good works.

Make A Daily Confession

I AM - God's greatest creation. I am full of power and creativity. I am fearfully and wonderfully made. My gifts will make a place for me and bring me before kings. I am created to perform good works and bring honor and glory to God.

I CAN - do all things through Christ who strengthens me. I can do exceedingly, abundantly, above all that I can ever think, or ask, according the power of God that is at work in me.

I WILL - fulfill the plan and purpose that God has for my life. I will suffer, but never surrender. I will rise above every obstacle and finish my course. I will be the recipient of riches, honor and long life.

I AM... full-of-beauty.
I am Beauty-full.

I AM... full-of-power.
I am Power-full.

I AM... full-of-wonder.
I am Wonder-full.

I AM... perfect... for God's Purpose.

* * *

Beauty-full Mothers & Grandmothers

I can remember the night my mother died like it was yesterday. For me, watching someone you love take their last breath is like watching the birth of a new baby. What was about to take place was about to change my life forever.

She had slipped into a coma and didn't seem to be in pain. Her chest moved up and down in a quiet rhythm. Her nostrils moved in and out with each breath. She took a deep breath, then another and another. Suddenly, she was still. My sister Marlene laid her head on my mother's chest to listen to her heart and at the same time comfort herself. We sang softly as the tears rolled down our faces.

"I'll fly away oh glory, I'll fly away. One glad morning when this life is over, I'll fly away."

Together we bathed my mothers' body before the rest of the family came into the room. She lay in the bed like a well loved, worn out rag doll. Her head was bald from the chemotherapy. The cancer had ravished her body leaving behind her thin, drawn remains. Her arms and legs were covered with black and blue marks from IV's and blood transfusions. But to me, at that moment, when we washed her face and covered her head with a soft blue cap, I have never seen her looked more beauty-full.

My mother was a simple woman who lived a quiet, yet extraordinary life. You will never find the name of Barbara Louise Prunty written down in the Hall of Fame, and that's just the way she would have wanted it.

They called the house that I grew-up in "Hotel Prunty" because the lights were always on and the front door was always open. Anybody in the neighborhood could sit down at our dinner table. Anybody who didn't have a place to stay could live at our house for as long as they needed to be there.

My mother was a nurse and she took care of everybody in the neighborhood, including the dogs and cats who had either been hit by a car or fallen out of a tree.

I can remember the night a battered woman named Rose came to our house seeking refuge from her crazy husband. When the man came looking for Rose and her children, my mother stood on the front porch with a shovel in her hands and dared him to come any closer.

"Do you want me to call daddy?" I asked my mother. "No!" she replied. "Don't call daddy, call the undertaker." The man left and never came back. Rose and her children lived with us for two years while she went back to school and found a job. Another lady asked my mother to baby-sit her little boy and came back three years later.

At night she worked as head nurse in the Delivery Room at a nearby hospital. She worked nights so she could be at home with her children during the day. Whenever there was an unwanted baby in the nursery where she worked, she would find a home for it before Social Service could be contacted. I have many cousins who were left in the hospital where my mother worked. Someone in my family would always adopt them.

Mom took care of the sick, defended the helpless, gave shelter to the battered and homeless, while caring for her family all at the same time. She spoiled her grandchildren shamelessly.

"Mom why are you and daddy spending all your money on your grandchildren," I would ask from time to time. "Every child is entitled to a childhood," she would always reply.

If ever there was a woman who could be the model and standard for beauty, it was my mother. She was indeed **beauty-full and full-of-beauty.** I dedicate this poem to her memory.

Before I Let You Go

I'm angry and I don't want the bracelet that you said would
be mine!
There's so much to live for and now there's so little time.
Your hair is all gone and you struggle
for each breath.
Could it be my darling Mother that we loved you to death?
You've taught me more things than I realize I know.
But I need more instructions before I let you go.
Like, what should I do to break up a family fight?
Only you knew for sure who was wrong and who was right.
How will I learn to forgive the deepest hurts
Co-sign for loans, share the house, give my shirt?
How will I keep the children from making
mistakes?
And where is the recipe for your gingerbread cake?
When daddy's spirits are down, how can I tell?
And what pill should I give Miss Margaret when her legs
start to swell?
I'm not strong like you, I could never
fill your shoes.
I know what you would say...
take my medicine and pay my dues.

Do you want me to rock you and sing
Amazing Grace?
Wipe the teardrops from your eyes and kiss your pretty face?
I'm so glad that as your spirit rises and leaves me here
below,
I had a chance to say I love you,
before I let you go.

* * *

My grandmother, Sadie Bell Campbell, had a different kind of beauty. While my mother liked the simple things, my grandmother was more flamboyant. On Sunday mornings, she wore wide flowered hats and long white gloves. Her silver mink stole would be draped over her arm as she took one last glance in the hall mirror before singing out, "Let's go children... it's time for church."

Grandmother gave her children and grandchildren a sense of dignity and self-esteem during a time when being Black wasn't viewed as beautiful. I grew-up in the middle of a violent, nonviolent, civil rights struggle. I still remember sitting next to her dressed in pink taffeta and wearing white gloves as Marion Anderson performed her farewell concert. "No other Negro woman has ever been on this stage," my grandmother whispered with pride.

On another occasion, just one look at my grandmother's smiling face made a man relinquish his seat so she could be comfortable while Dr. Martin Luther King delivered a stirring message. "Sugar works better than vinegar," she smiled at me.

On that same night riding home on the trolley car, a White man who had a little too much to drink started shouting and calling Dr. King degrading names. I tried to be the dignified lady that my grandmother had raised me to be, but in a burst of rage my sister Marlene and I started hitting the man over the head with our umbrellas. My grandmother was very disappointed in our behavior, but I think she understood.

She learned to drive when she was fifty years old. Claimed she had places to go and things to do! Grandmom could fix anything that was broken and transform an ordinary house into a palace with finds from a secondhand store or pieces of furniture and art given to her by one of her grateful White employers.

She played the piano and recited poetry. James Weldon Johnson was one of her favorites. On Sunday afternoons after dinner, my brother, sisters, aunts and uncles would gather around the piano for a private performance.

I learned how to pray kneeling down next to her, my fingers would be clutched together and resting on her beautiful lavender bed spread.

"Once I had a dream," she said before praying with me one night. "I was walking across a field and suddenly their was a dark cloud. I knew it was the devil coming after me. I began to say... 'Our Father who art in heaven, hallowed be thy name...' Suddenly, the dark cloud disappeared and the sun was shining again. Your Heavenly Father will hear you whenever you call His name," she said.

She looked at me and smiled. Word by word she taught me "The Lord's Prayer."

On the day that she died, she asked to be bathed and dressed. She sat in her wing backed chair and finished her dinner. One hour later she died with the same quiet dignity that had been the trademark of her life. She was the beauty-full lady who made a real lady out of her Tomboy granddaughter. She was the beauty-full lady who introduced me to poetry, music and art. She was the beauty-full lady who introduced me to God. I dedicate these words to her memory.

Grandmom Sadie

Her words sparkled like a jewelry box opening wide to
reveal its precious gems.
Her house was my classroom, her eyes always teaching me
how to place the linen napkin in my lap and drink from
crystal goblets.
Sunday was a day of gathering her offspring together to
inspect her children's gardens.
With a gentle touch, she pulled up weeds of wrong thinking
and planted new seed.
The women held court at her kitchen table waiting for the
weekly report of who died, who was expecting
and private matters that could not be spoken to anyone
beyond those walls.
When her hands became too old to bake her apple pies, she
whispered to me the secret ingredients that bind families
together and blind them to one another's faults.
Her bedroom smelled like God lived there. An angel reciting
The Lord's Prayer smiled at me from a plaque that was
nailed to her lilac wallpaper.
Two packs of kool-aide and a loaf of Wonder bread she
wrote on a piece of paper and sent me off to the
grocery store.
When I returned, she had gone to be with the Lord.

* * *

Shelly Jones, my great-grandmother was as different
from grandmother Sadie Bell, as day is to night. She was fiery
and very eccentric. It was not unusual for her to wave her
shotgun at anyone she suspected of stealing one of her prize
hens or a jug of her homemade wine that she kept in the shed.

When the family left Philadelphia and headed for the Eastern Shore of Maryland for the summer, I couldn't wait to stay at Grandmom Shelly's house. I loved the smell of her old parlor where she kept her big mahogany organ. The best thing about staying with great-grandmother was the stories that she told. The two of us would sit in the kitchen by the wood stove drinking ice tea while she told one of her famous tales.

Her ghost stories would send a chill up my spine. But one of my favorites was a tale about old man Joe who broke into her wine shed. Little did he know that she had filled one of the bottles with Ex-lax. Everybody knew he was guilty, because he stayed in the outhouse (bathroom for the younger folks) for two days.

My family members always teased me saying I was just like Shelly Jones when I was telling a story. The gift of storytelling ran in my family. My mother could go to the market and come back with a mini-series about something that happened on the way home. Grandmother Sadie was more of a poet when she told stories. She knew how to paint beautiful pictures that would take us away from the small dismal street that we lived on to a beautiful mansion in the sky. But great-grandmother Shelly was my favorite, out of all my beauty-full storytellers. I dedicate this poem to my great-grandmother Shelly.

The Storyteller

There's a place in my mind that I like to visit from
time to time.
Grandma Shelly is telling a story that has me on the
edge of my seat
but she suddenly stops...
would you believe to fix something to eat!

The biscuits are brown and the butter is dripping hot
But I can't take one bite,
til I know why Walter got shot!
Her words are like fuel on the fire of mind.
She pauses, she whispers, leaving me suspended in time.
She studies my face, then laughs out loud.
Girl, you got the look of a storyteller
and that makes me proud!
Be sure to tell about that mean old rooster that gave your
brother a fit
chased him around the yard til he ran him in a ditch.
There was the camp meetings, the homecomings
and grandaddy's passing.
He wasn't even cold before his kin was taking
without even asking.
That night I went to the attic and rattled some chains.
By dawn the house was empty,
they relinquished their claims.
If laughter's the medicine that brings healing to our soul,
then it was Grandma Shelly's stories,
that kept our family whole.

* * *

The list of women who gave me life would not be complete without adding the name of my great-great-grandmother Cordelia Jones. My great uncle Roma said that my youngest daughter Theresa has Cordelia's small frame and copper brown skin color. I'm not sure what she really looked like, but I do know that she was a *beauty-full* woman of prayer and power.

Grandmother Sadie paid me the greatest compliment when she said that I prayed like Cordelia. I am told that every morning my great-great-grandmother would go to the front door of the house open it wide and begin to pray to the Lord. Her words were always the same. "Lord, bless my children and bless my children's children. May all the generations of my family forever proclaim Jesus as Lord."

I thank the Lord for Cordelia's example of godliness. The torch has passed and like my great-great-grandmother. I pray for my family each day. I begin by saying: "Lord bless my children and bless my children's children. May all the generations of my family forever proclaim Jesus as Lord."

This poem is for you Cordelia.

Cordelia's Prayer

Wisdom perches on the branches of my grandmothers words.
She speaks softly as the winds of change blow against her
honey brown face.
She embroiders life with golden threads
and looks at me with loving eyes.
"I keep you right here," she whispers,
pointing to her heart.
There is a quiet presence in her sunlit room.
She is not alone.
She rehearses my petition, seals it with her tears.
On wings of faith it flies toward heaven.
As surely as butterflies rise to meet the morning sun
and raindrops give life to seed buried in the earth,
I know that God hears her voice
and it is done.

* * *

Many of you may not have been blessed to experience the love of a mother, grandmother or great-grandmother. But African Americans come from a wonder-full heritage called extended family. If a child didn't have a mother or grand-mother, the old lady next door, or one of the mothers at church would take her in her arms and make her a part of her family. My doors have always been open to children seeking refuge. It is the tradition that I grew up with and I wouldn't have had it any other way.

My cousin Starletta came to live with us when she was seventeen and I was sixteen. Her brother Buddy was al-ready staying at our house when she arrived. Her parents had gone through a bitter divorce. It was now up to the extended family to step in and make sure that Starletta and Buddy had the love and protection they needed.

My two younger sisters were a year apart in age so they did everything together. When cousin Starletta parked her possessions on the vacant twin bed in my third floor bed-room. It felt like I not only had a sister to hang out with but a new best friend.

We did everything together, including going out on double dates. I can still remember trying to sneak into the house long after our curfew. Mom was sitting on the front porch waiting for us. She lined us up in the living room along with the young men who had taken us out and read us the riot act.

Because of grandparents, aunts and uncles, Starletta was able to cope with the problems she was having with her parents. At our house she could be a teenager again, instead of a mediator between her mom and dad. Star taught me how to dance, I taught her how to sew. She talked me into going to nursing school and I encouraged her to be an actress. She in-troduced me to Thunderbird wine and I taught her how to smoke. It was the circle of family that kept us both on the right track. Mom would sit with us for hours giving advice about education and boyfriends. To this very day Starletta and I act more like sisters than cousins.

We must keep this tradition alive. If there's a young girl in your neighborhood or church who seems to need love and nurturing, why not embrace her and make her your adopted daughter. Then, when you are too old to care for yourself, you will have daughters and granddaughters who will be there to give back the love and care that you once gave to them.

If you are a young woman who lives in a city away from your family, or your mother is no longer living, I would encourage you to find a beauty-full mothering woman in your church or community. Her wisdom and experience will help you make good decisions. Her encouragement will cheer you on as you strive to reach your goals. Her words of affirmation will make you feel good about yourself, even when you've gained a little weight. I dedicate this poem to those special "moms" in our lives.

My Second Mom

She moaned when she prayed:
"Lord keep her safe from harm"
It was strange how her embrace felt just like my
mother's arms.
Where did she come from? I thought to my self.
Why was she suddenly there when I needed her help?
Did she stop by heaven to chat for a while?
Did my grandmother whisper,
"please take care of my child."
The food from her table took me back to a place where I
watched steam rise from the greens while daddy said grace.
"Miss Pearl," I said. "May I please use your phone?"
"Just call me mom, Sugar... and make yourself at home."
I kicked off my shoes, and wiggled my tired toes,
How I found this lady, God only knows.
I did just like she said and made myself at home.

I smiled, cause at last I had found
a mom of my own.

* * *

The Old Landmarks

I can still remember Aretha Franklin's gospel album, *Amazing Grace.* Over and over I loved to hear her sing at the top of her lungs, "Let us all go back to the old landmarks... let us all go back to the old landmarks!"

Although it was one of the familiar gospel songs that my choir use to sing when I was very young, I never really understood what the words meant. Like many explosive gospel songs, the message often gets lost in the excitement of the music. I still have visions of women wiping their tears and trying to calm themselves down with a fan from the Harrison and Ross Mortuary as the worship gained momentum. Each time the organ hit a high pitch, or the man with the big gravelly voice sang out, "Thank You Jesus," the pandemonium would start. The preacher would try to calm the people down, but the organ and drum would stir them up all over again. For me, church is one of the "Old Landmarks" that reminds me of how African-Americans survived.

There were no family therapists in the neighborhood where I grew up. And if there were, nobody had any money for treatment. When the stress became too great, the bills piled up, or some other problem that seemed to be overwhelming came up, it was all sorted out as the organ played and the preacher preached. Children giggled and bourgeois ladies groaned as the beauty-full older women danced their problems away. Wigs fell off, they ran around the church, or jumped over the pews releasing the strain and the pain. I find it interesting that all the books on stress reduction recommend walking, bike riding or some type of physical exercise. The reason is simple. When the body is under stress, it produces a substance called adrenaline. This chemical gives the body superhuman strength to run away or fight off physical attacks. The adrenaline is burned off during the struggle. If the attack is psychological and not physical, the adrenaline remains in the body and becomes poisonous to the system. Excess adrenaline in the body can be linked to nervous breakdowns, high blood pressure and heart attacks. The only way to burn off the negative effects of adrenaline is physical exercise.

People shouting, jumping and dancing in church is a perfect way to release the buildup of stress and the negative effects of adrenaline. In the days when dancing and shouting were the norm in Black churches, suicides, nervous breakdowns and people with guns killing each other only happened on rare occasions. God worked miracles for the beauty-full women who dared to sing His praises. Food was on the table, their husbands found work and their children went to college and grew up to live a better life.

The Old Testament of the Bible tells us to build a memorial stone for those events in our history that tell the story of God's goodness to His people. Then when the children ask about the "landmarks" or monuments that are connected to our history, we are to tell them the story of "how we got over." This will teach them to appreciate and respect God and respect all that our forefathers had to endure.

Unfortunately, too many young African-American women have not been the recipients of the recipes, remedies, crafts and wisdom of our African-American heritage. I never thought I would live to see a day where our elders would be disrespected with "back-talk," and allowed to be on a first name basis with little children. Many young people do not know names of Martin Luther King, Jr., Harriet Tubman or Jesus Christ. The wisdom and religion of their elders is laughed at, while a generation of young people race toward destruction of every kind. Wedding gifts are not even unwrapped before the marriage has disintegrated.

The beauty of our elders is that they are able to point to the "old landmarks," that have given us the wisdom we need to keep our marriages alive, keep our families together and raise decent and power-full children.

Whenever I wasn't getting along with my husband, I can still remember my grandmother saying:

"When it comes to men honey, sometimes it's better to be quiet than right."

When my work schedule became hectic and my mother thought my children weren't getting enough attention, I can still remember her words:

"Love can stretch a lot further than money. Spend more time with them kids, girl."

During the seventies, many African-Americans bought into the philosophy of "self-realization," "self-actualization," "me, my and I," "looking out for number one" and, "I need my personal space" era.

Instead of living in the tradition of extended families where grandma and grandpa stayed around to support and affirm young married couples and their children, they left the "old landmark" of living under one roof, next door, or in the same neighborhood. Big Mama and Papa were sent to a senior citizens home, while the younger ones moved to the "big city" to seek fame and fortune. With the removal of close family ties and "grandma's hands," we lost the medicine that keeps a young family healthy and strong.

Divorce, working mothers, absentee fathers and scattered family members are a perfect formula for the destruction of a race. We make more money, but most of it is paid out in "sin taxes." Sin taxes are simply money that must be paid out because we have failed or neglected to raise up a generation of people who are living productive and respectable lives. We are forced to pay for more prisons because of the rising number or young criminals. We are forced to pay for Aid To Dependent Children so teenage mothers will be able to care for their babies. With no older women around, young Black women who would have given their beauty-full babies life, flush them down the drains of the abortion clinics. There was a time in the African-American community when babies were thought of as gifts from God. If they didn't have a momma or daddy, some beauty-full Black woman was always around to raise that child along with her own. Even though we lived in a society that didn't value us, we still valued one another.

Robberies are up because nobody stays at home, and our senior citizens have been institutionalized. When I was young, grandpa, grandma and auntie were always in and out of the house. The people who are breaking into houses today would have been the same people who stayed out of trouble, because someone would have been in the house to fix them a plate of greens and cornbread and to give them some good advice and encouragement.

The beauty-full women who became our "aunties" and "play mommas" were all the policing we needed. I can still remember ditching school and heading downtown to see a movie. I was fourteen and I thought I was grown until my Aunt Alice (not a real aunt but one of my mother's friends) spotted me walking down the street smoking cigarettes. She grabbed my cigarettes and marched me back home, scolding me the whole way. When we got to my street, my real Aunt Mootsie was standing out front. Aunt Alice told her what I did. Aunt Mootsie held off and hit me as hard as she could. By the time my mother got home I was wishing that I had never been born. Needless to say, it took the whole village to make me the woman that I am today.

We must help our younger women recognize and respect the gifts that are hiding in older women. I can still remember being in a teacher training class at my church. Each Sunday, one of the members of the class had to prepare a lesson. One particular Sunday, the task of preparing the lesson fell on an older lady named Mother Mary Johnson. She was well into her seventies. The lines in her face folded back like a dark velvet curtain when she smiled. Her words had a musical tone like she was about to sing. But on this particular day, as she stood up with her Bible in her hand, she appeared to be nervous and uneasy. She tried to read a passage of scripture, but again and again stumbled over the words. She squinted her eyes as she looked over her well worn glasses, but her presentation only grew worse. The younger people in the class seemed to be bored and annoyed as Mother Johnson continued. Suddenly she stopped reading and closed the book.

"My eyes ain't that good anymore," she began. "And I never was much of a reader. But if you give me a few minutes I can tell you from my heart what God has done for me."

For the next twenty minutes the old woman with the velvet skin shared the wisdom of the ages. Tears ran down the faces of the listeners as she talked about singing, praying and weeping in the cotton fields of Mississippi. We were transported to the prayer meetings that took place under the moonlight skies of the deep south. She explained how the women stood by their men and protected them from being murdered by the Klan. Her closing words etched into my memory forever.

Mother Johnson looked at everyone in the room. I thought I could hear her humming softly to herself before she spoke. "Many nights I prayed that I would live to see the day when my children and grandchildren would have enough food to eat and be able to get a decent education. All of you are my children. That's why I came to this class," she smiled. "So I can see how the young ones was doing. I can see you all doing alright... you all dressed up serving the Lord and reading real good. I guess my prayers have been answered. I can get me some rest now."

We sat quietly in our seats trying to absorb the love that had poured over us like warm molasses. Mother Johnson picked up her things and left the room still humming to herself as she closed the door.

Older women must see themselves as the history books and the learning trees for young women to sit beneath and find wisdom. Younger women should be open to new concepts and new ideas, but they should still cherish those tried and tested practices of their elders. If at all possible, stay close to your family members. They will be an anchor in the storm for you and your family. If you don't live near family members, join a church where you personally, and your family, can become a part of a larger and protective family group. Together we stand, divided we fall. Keep standing!

* * *

Beauty-full Men in my Life

Any woman who has been fortunate enough to have known beauty-full men is blessed indeed. The first man that I loved and idolized was my grandfather, *Melgratton Campbell*. He was a hard worker and very strict. He loved his family to the core. If you did something wrong on Monday, he made an appointment to spank you on Friday and he always kept his appointments. During the summer months, he loaded the children into the back of his pickup truck and headed for the family farm in Lynchburg, Virginia. I can remember him curing ham in the smokehouse and lifting me up high enough to pick apples from the tree in the front yard.

My favorite memory was sitting on his knee while he sang to me. I can still remember the words. The melody was like a down-home Muddy Waters blues song. In his deep southern accent he would start singing:

"You're my snaffu rastus, my pork chop Alabama - bam. I say, you my snaffu rastus, my pretty little Alabama bam. I love you, I love you, I love you, my preeeety little pork chop, Alaaabama bammmm!"

Little did I realize that the man that I later married would have my grandfather's same personality, facial features, coffee coloring and a deep southern accent. The image of what love looked like was forever etched into my heart by this loving man who called me his little pork chop, Ala-bama-bam.

I only have vague memories of my natural father. Although my mother never said an unkind word about him, I know that he was an alcoholic who drank himself to death. I remember seeing him twice in my life. Once he came to visit me. I must have been six or seven years old. My brother and I sat next to him on a bar stool while he drank whiskey all afternoon. The second, and last time I saw him, I was grown and pregnant with my daughter Theresa. He died the year after she was born. I didn't attend his funeral. I think I was more bitter than I realized at the time. If I could see him now, I would thank him for giving me life. In spite of his faults, I know that he was very gifted and God used the gifts that were in him to make me the special person that I am today.

You may feel bitterness toward your natural father and wonder why God didn't give you a better parent, but God recognized the good qualities in your natural father that would be needed to make you success-full and special. Shaquille O'Neal was abandoned by his father, but it would be a good guess that his father's genes contributed to his success as an athlete.

When I was four years old, my father abandoned my mother, leaving her with two children to raise and another one on the way.

Alvin Prunty, my "real dad," came to my mother's rescue a year after my youngest sister was born. He was the man who provided for her and took care of us like we were his own children. He came from a broken home and joined the Army when he was only fifteen. He later said that when he married my mother, he married into the family he never had. My stepfather loved my grandfather almost as much as he loved my mother. He was determined to do his best to give us the home and the security that he never had.

Dad checked our homework, talked with our teachers, taught us Spanish as a second language, and let us make peanut butter and bologna sandwiches when mom wasn't around. He had a passion for books and encouraged me to read. He would sit in the living room reading to himself. My brother and I would be on the edge of our seats as he shared one of the chapters from the book. Suddenly, he would stop right at the most exciting part.

"If you want to know what happened, you'll have to read it yourself," he would say, leaving the book on the table. He paid us a nickel a piece when we read the funny papers without making a mistake. But I love him the most for stirring my imagination. When my mother wanted me to be a nurse, he encouraged me to follow my love for creative writing.

Adam McFaddin, my late husband, was without a doubt the single most painful and powerful experience in my entire life. In our eight years of marriage, there is little doubt that his life and death also marked the life and death of a big part of Terri McFaddin.

I was twenty two years old when I met Adam McFaddin. He was thirty three. We were married two months after we met. He gave me everything a woman could want. He was my friend, my protector, the provider of everything that I ever desired. He picked my clothes, discovered that I was wearing the wrong shoe size, and taught me how to cook gumbo. He was my mentor and the molder of my personality as a woman.

He was a shrewd businessman. He had two automobile franchises, as well as other business interests. We worked together on everything. I handled his advertising and wrote his business proposals. He was a meticulous dresser and a connoisseur of the good life. We would get away on weekends with the kids just to love one another and to talk things out. We planned our work and worked our plan. The plans for the expansion of his domain were still on the drawing board when he found out he was dying from cancer.

"What are you going to do with your life when I'm gone?" he asked one morning at the breakfast table. The question hit me like a ton of bricks. I couldn't imagine life without him, and sometimes I still can't. Although he battled the disease for three years, when he finally died, it set off shock waves inside of me that lasted for years. He passed away on a Sunday evening. He had been restless all day. Looking back, I can see that he was trying to mask the intensity of his pain.

The doctors made it clear that they had done everything possible, and now Adam was in God's hands. As we sat there talking that afternoon, I realized why he was still alive. He never said the words, but suddenly I knew that he didn't think I was strong enough to make it without him. In many respects he was right. But suddenly I felt like someone was speaking through me. I still don't know how I found the words that poured out of my heart.

My voice was trembling and I could hardly breathe as I tried to speak. "Adam, I know you're struggling to live because the children and I need you so much, but I'm stronger than you think.. and with God's help, I know I can make it."

For the first time that day he seemed to relax. I sat on the side of the bed and held him in my arms. I rocked him for hours until he stopped breathing.

In the months that followed I had two nervous breakdowns. I lost every dime that we had worked for in court battles with my husband's business partners. I was too naive to understand how to fight for what belonged to me and my children. But through it all, I learned from him the lesson of perseverance and determination.

After I crawled into a ball for the last time crying out

to God, asking Him, "why me?" things began to change for the better. Without really knowing what happened, the Lord began to heal my broken heart and broken life. I sat on the couch one night looking at a stack of bills, most of which were marked urgent or final notice. My hands were trembling as I tried to find the courage to deal with what might be waiting inside of those big white envelopes. My childhood friend Maria sat next to me for encouragement.

"Don't try to tackle the whole thing all at once. Let's open one letter a day," she said.

I was fighting back the tears as I opened the first envelope. It read as follows:

"Dear Terri: We have been trying for months to reach you. Congratulations on the release of the song you wrote for the Whispers. We have enclosed your contract and a check for five thousand dollars."

By the time I finished opening the first pile of mail, I had almost ten thousand dollars. I didn't know the Lord then, but looking back I can clearly see that He knew me and was with me.

My husband asked me what would I do with my life after he was gone. At the time, I didn't have an answer to that question. How could I know that two years later I would sign a contract with Motown records and became a successful songwriter. It was nothing short of a miracle that I was allowed to make a good living while being at home during the day with my two children. Later I was called into the ministry, which was a bigger surprise than signing a songwriter's contract.

The pain that I went through was long and intense. But it was the suffering that brought my inner-beauty and talent to the surface. With every Gold record and Grammy Award, I could feel Adam smiling. I hope that as the mother of his children, I have made him proud.

* * *

It makes me sad to think of all of the strife that goes on between African American men and women. I am grateful for the kind and loving Black men who dispelled the myth that Black women and men are not sensitive and supportive of one another.

From the beginning of time, the greatest strategy for destroying a race of people is dividing and conquering. The slave traders flourished in Africa as a result of Europeans creating conflicts between the tribes. Once a war broke out, the Europeans supplied guns in exchange for prisoners of tribal wars. This same ruthless approach was taken to divide and destroy Black families in America.

In the post-slavery era, women were told over and over again that Black men where lazy and irresponsible. In the same breath, Whites refused to grant Black men the licenses needed to operate businesses such as blacksmiths, carpentry or other respectable trades. They were forced to do the most menial jobs or not work at all. If a Black man found a way to prosper in the face of adversity, White racist were always in the shadows plotting his downfall. In their heart-of-hearts, Black men have always desired to care for their families and make Black women feel beauty-full, loved and protected. But without the power and stability that comes from having a job or owning a business, a Black man cannot feel good about himself. Therefore, he cannot make the women and children in his life feel beauty-full and special.

In spite of the facade of "equal opportunities" for African American men, it is simply that... a facade. My husband was one of the first African American men to have a General Motors Automobile franchise. On the outside, it looked like things were going smoothly. In reality, it was a constant struggle against the never ending plots of corporate heads and bankers who wanted to prove that a Black man could not succeed in business.

I can still remember my husband holding a gun on a banker who plotted to destroy his line of credit.

"Everything that my family and I have worked for is tied up in this dealership," my husband told the man. "If I go down, I'm taking you with me."

Overnight, things changed for the better.

* * *

The plan that God had for man to experience the abundant life is spelled out in the book of Genesis 1:21: *And God said to them (Adam and Eve) be fruitful and multiply. Subdue the earth and have dominion over every living thing.*

Fruitfulness: Success and financial gain
Multiply: To reproduce - build families
Subdue: To conquer and bring into subjection
Dominion: To rule and govern

Because of these mandates from God, the natural struggles between "fallen men" have always been centered around money, power and sex.

The first chapter in the book of Exodus gives a classic example of men caught in a life and death struggle for power and dominion.

The story begins with the Egyptian King who is called Pharaoh. He was extremely concerned with the rapid population growth of the Children of Israel. His fears were centered around the fact that the Israelites out numbered the Egyptians. If a war broke out, they would be in a position to overthrow Pharaoh's government. With this in mind, Pharaoh devised a plan to work the men beyond their strength, and to make their lives so miserable that they would grow weak and die.

Unfortunately, the plan backfired. The Bible tells us that the more the Children of Israel were oppressed the more they multiplied. Sound familiar? In a final attempt to protect Egypt's position, Pharaoh commanded that all of the male babies should be put to death. The females did not represent the same kind of threat that the males did. The females would grow up with a desire to marry and have babies, but the males would grow up with the desire to rule and take territory from other rulers.

It is clear to me that the breakdown of the family structure, unemployment, and the availability of drugs and guns are the tools designed to bring about the destruction of an entire race of people. Black women have always been fearful and protective of their husbands and sons. Regardless of wealth, education or prominence, Black women still pace the floor at night wondering if a husband, brother or son is just running late or has been arrested, assaulted or killed by the police.

History gives us a clear example of the fear that one powerful group of males has over a less powerful group. Even though the Israelites did not have the power of the Egyptians, they still represented a threat because of their ability to "multiply" and produce a large number of male children. It only took one male child who was empowered by God to change the history of a nation. His name was Moses. He lead the revolt against the Egyptians, took their wealth and lead his people into the Promise Land. For many of the same reasons, powerfull Black men are viewed as a threat to the White power structure in America.

The tribal wars continue in the headliner case, Rodney King vs. Stacey Koones and the Foothill police. The city of Los Angeles burned to the ground in revenge for what was viewed as a tribal injustice.

Once again, the whole nation was glued to their television as Johnny Cochran and O.J. Simpson faced Mark

Furhman and Marsha Clarke. From the polls that were taken it was clear that the trial was not about murder, but race. Statistics showed that, right or wrong, each tribe was clearly rooting for their own.

The O.J. Simpson trial became so sensational because it represented the age old struggle between White male vs. Black male. In this trial of the century, the White male power structure struggled to send the message, that the most successful Black men are in reality, out of control savages, pretending to be civilized. Given the right circumstances, a Black man will always revert to his base instincts which was demonstrated in the brutal death of Nicole Brown Simpson.

Somehow, with all of the demonic forces that have come against African-American families, we have still managed to find enough faith and love to hold on to one another.

It was a brother named Ernie Sprinkles who helped me recover from a nervous breakdown. He never misused me, or tried to take advantage of my vulnerability. He just watched over me until I was strong again. I will always remember the men in my life as heroes who are beauty-full, wonder-full and power-full. I especially give thanks for the following men:

• *Pastor E. V. Hill* - For introducing me to Jesus.
• *S. Harry Young* - My friend and brother. Words could never express how much I thank God for Harry.
• *Frank Wilson* - For being a faithful brother and friend. I thank him and his wife Bunny for being Godparents to my daughters.
• *Tom Skinner* - Who is now with the Lord. For challenging me intellectually and spiritually. I thank him and his wife Barbara for being Godparents to Theresa, and helping her through college.
• *Todd Prunty* - My nephew. From the time he was a child he protected his cousin Theresa from all the people who laughed

at her because she was different.

- *Paul Goodnight* - For helping me to discover my inner-beauty. For using his art to immortalize the beauty of African women around the world.
- *Philip Bailey* - My faithful brother and friend. We are joined at the heart.
- *Andrae' Crouch* - A heart bigger than Texas. My Pastor, brother and friend.
- *Charles Johnson* - A son and a friend. For always having my back.
- *Ollie Brown* - For always watching over me.
- *Paul Jackson, Jr.* - Like a son, watching over me and praying for me.
- *Larry Brown* - My guardian angel.
- *Leonard Caston* - My friend. He made a songwriter out of me.
- *Richard Phillips* - My uncle. Solid as a rock.
- *Adam McFaddin Ballard* - My grandson. My gift from God.
- *Anthony Ballard* - My grandson. My gift from God.
- *Rick Ballard* - He is the son-in-law from heaven.

* * *

When a Man Loves a Woman

It was in the early spring of 1993 when we first met. We walked along the windy streets in the direction of a small cafe. We talked, but we weren't really listening to what was being said. I could feel his eyes as he studied my face. My hair felt three inches longer, my body felt ten pounds lighter and without a doubt, his smile melted my years away.

I think we drank peppermint tea and stopped in a gallery to look at paintings. The only thing I really remember was the rhythm of our steps as we walked together, and my nervous laughter when his eyes implied that I was beautiful.

A very strange thing happened just as we were about to say good-bye. We were talking very casually when suddenly tears weld up in my eyes. He was startled. I might have been embarrassed, but didn't really care. How could he possibly know that it had been years since a man had looked at me with loving eyes and made me feel like I wasn't invisible anymore.

* * *

The love and affection of a caring man does more to make a woman feel beauty-full than all the makeup, weight loss programs, and hair stylists put together. One simple sentence from his lips, "I believe in you. I love you." Suddenly, she transformed into a flawless, invincible, confident woman.

Next to knowing Jesus Christ, being loved by a good man is the most precious gift that God could ever give to a woman. I don't ever remember seeing a bride that wasn't beauty-full. Once the groom fixes his eyes on his beloved and she takes that walk down the aisle, for that moment, she is the most beauty-full woman on earth.

Unfortunately, there are too many African American women who have never known the affirming passion of a man's love. The reason of course is the shortage of eligible men. Women of color are painfully aware of the men we have lost to drug addiction, homosexuality, incarceration and those who are just too afraid to commit. If ever there was a time for women to come together and pray our brothers out of the prisons of addiction, perversion and rage, it is now.

We must be sensitive to the struggles that Black men go through as it relates to employment, business opportunities and self-esteem. Be careful not to flaunt your success in the face of a brother who is struggling to survive. You both hold the keys to releasing one another's inner-beauty. By focusing on his "person" and not his "profession," you give him an opportunity to put his energy into discovering your inner beauty instead of being guarded and defensive about his own life.

We want our men to be husbands and fathers, but all too often they are afraid to take the plunge. Why? Because many of them were not raised with a positive male role model. Many of them were raised with no man in the house at all. How can you expect a man to picture himself as a husband or father when he really doesn't know how to be one?

I believe that the absence of good fathers in the home is one of the many reasons for the rise in crime among Black males. I also believe that missing fathers account for the increasing numbers of homosexuals and men who are fearful of being in a committed relationship with a woman.

The following brothers shared with me their concerns about being in a committed relationship.

Phil - A former professional athlete. He was powerful and confident, yet there was a side of him that was sensitive, and almost fragile as he began his story.

"I was the youngest in my family. I never really knew my father. The one time I remember meeting him was at my mother's funeral. He looked at me, grunted my name and walked away. I was devastated. I also felt rejected. But I wasn't as devastated as I was on the day that my mother died. It's been years, but I remember it like it was yesterday. She was my friend, my main girl. She was the one who loved me and gave me the confidence that I needed. But suddenly, she was gone."

"I went to live with my grandmother. She was full of love and showered it all on me. Because my older brother was a homosexual, she encouraged me to get involved in sports, do macho things and be responsible. But suddenly, she too became ill and passed away. My older brother was all I had left, but shortly after my grandmother's death, he died from AIDS."

"Now when I get involved with a woman, I just can't let myself get too close to her. I just can't bare the thought of losing another woman that I love."

"Maybe if I had been raised with my father around, I would have been more balanced. I wouldn't have been so emotional about my mother and grandmother. But I can't change what has already happened," he smiled.

"It seems like the relationships that I get involved in are designed to fail. I don't do it intentionally, but I guess I need to be with someone who I can lose, without going through anymore pain."

A woman in a relationship with Phil might not have the opportunity to understand the reason for the invisible wall that separates them. If she lacks confidence and self-esteem, she will quickly come to the conclusion that Phil's lack of commitment is because of something she lacks. Even if he takes the time to explain that his actions are not based on anything she is lacking as a woman, she is still haunted by feelings of rejection and inadequacy.

David - another handsome and seemingly eligible young man, finished college and went to work for a company that offered him a bright future in management. He advanced quickly and was looking forward to the day when he and his girlfriend would settle down and raise a family. Just before the wedding of his best friend, there was a investigation at his job. He was charged with embezzlement and sent to jail.

"For the first time I understood what slavery was like when I had to strip down and spread my legs like a worthless animal."

While he was incarcerated, he discovered that he had been set up by a White racist in upper management. David was so angry that he plotted to have the man killed. A friend talked some sense into him and he did not go through with his plan. By divine intervention, the criminal charges were finally dropped.

"I had to rebuild my entire life," he explained. "My girlfriend went through hell. She tried to stick with me through the whole ordeal, but I drove her crazy. We finally broke up. I've never been in a serious relationship since that incident. Deep inside, I'm still very angry. Life is too uncertain for Black men. I don't want to get involved in any more commitments that I may not be able to keep."

The struggles that Black men go through are very

real. Too many of them have been wounded by fathers who
were caught up in their own struggles with racism and unemployment. Too many of them were abused or abandoned by
fathers who were broken by a system designed to break them
and their families.

John - shared with me a conversation that he had
with his alcoholic father just before his father's death.

"My dad told me that he drank because he was angry
with the way things were." He grew up in the South where
Black men had to step off the sidewalk if a White person was
coming down the street. He moved to Chicago in the early
50's thinking things would be better, but nothing really changed.
Always being the last one hired and the first one fired, he turned
to drinking and abusing the family he loved, which became the
expression of his rage.

"I guess I never wanted to get married because I'm
afraid that if I'm not successful in my profession, I may become like him."

Watching the tears role down this brother's face was
a reminder that on the surface, Black men seem to have it all
together. They can seem cool and aloof but underneath, they
are simply trying to keep a safe distance because they still hurt
and they still cry inside.

For women, marriage and having a baby are the ultimate expressions of her femininity. For men, their manhood is
expressed through the money they earn and the power they can
exercise. Second only to a man's sexual performance is the
ability to provide and protect his family. This is the ultimate
expression of his manhood. Without money and some degree
of control over his life, a man views himself as impotent and
weak.

Many Black men are afraid that a wife will become a
competitor rather than a partner, or the challenges of living in a

racist society may keep him from providing for his family. His wife might become more successful and leave him in the dust. He also worries that she may be smarter and able to out think him. He may have fears that he may not measure up to her sexual expectations. He has fantasies of losing his freedom and his right to be in control of his own life. These are just a few of the fears that men express to me on a regular basis.

We must first understand that we have a problem. Then we can begin to look for solutions. Too many women want to jump in bed today and go find a wedding ring tomorrow. Being in a committed relationship that works takes two very serious and mature people. Take the time to develop a friendship. Establish mutual respect and trust for one another. Don't play games. Listen to his heart. Learn his strengths and weaknesses. Love him for who he is and not for who you want him to be.

We need African American men to add beauty to our lives. We need African American men to be our husbands and fathers who will remain in the home to protect and provide for our children. It is only when our families are intact with the husband as the provider and protector, and the wife as the nurturer and encourager, will the full spectrum of our beauty be fully seen.

The shortage of good men has set off a chain reaction of confusion for women. Many single women think they are manless because of something they are lacking or doing wrong. Others have buried themselves in their careers, or turned to other women for companionship.

"If only I was younger, more attractive, had a better job, lived in a different city, or didn't have kids." These are just a few of the reasons why many women believe they are alone. But the truth of the matter is that there is nothing wrong with you, except that you may be unprepared for the role of becoming a success-full wife.

In light of these challenges, women must first be sensitive to the society that we live in and secondly, learn the fine art of recognizing a good man if one should come her way. Just as you want men to see the beauty that is on the inside of you, look beneath his surface and into the heart and soul of a man. All too often I hear single women say:

"The man of my dreams must be tall, with broad shoulders, wavy hair and lots of money." But they fail to notice how often "Mr. Fly Guy" never seems to be around when you really need him. If you make the mistake of allowing 'a roll in the sheets' to blind you to the truth, in the end, you may find yourself robbed of your beauty and self-esteem. One woman reported that she was robbed of everything, including her life savings.

All too often Black men get mixed signals about what Black women really want.

"Black women don't want nice guys!" one man argued with me. "When I treat a woman with love and respect, she thinks I'm weak. If I act like a dog, then I'm the man."

This may be true to some extent, but I still believe that there are women who truly desire to be loved and appreciated by a kind and tenderhearted man. Remember, if you are hung up on the packaging, you just might miss the gift on the inside.

What makes a man beauty-full? I'm so glad you asked. The following are some of the qualities you should be looking for:

1. He loves God and loves his family.
2. He is not emotionally unstable, controlling or insecure.
3. He is ambitious and has a solid work history.
4. He is not involved in drugs or criminal activities.
5. He is not promiscuous or involved in homosexuality.
6. He is honest and trustworthy.

7. He does not feel threatened by your success.
8. He is responsible and takes care of his obligations.
9. He is affectionate and not afraid of commitment.
10. He is protective and treats you with respect.
11. He is not intimidated by living in a racist society.
12. If he has children, he is involved and supportive.

Whatever you do, don't take anything for granted. He may use his charm to convince you that he is something that he's not. Be sure to check his story out before you get too involved.

* * *

The married woman has a completely different kind of row to hoe. It's almost like performing in a circus. She has to learn how to balance and juggle her duties as a wife, mother, career woman; his family and her family; while at the same time maintaining her inner and outer beauty.

One of the biggest mistakes that a woman can make is to think that after she says "I DO," then I don't have to dress up all the time. I don't have to set goals for myself. I can sleep with my big pink rollers. I don't have to fix fancy meals, or have sex by the fireplace. I can just be me.

One angry husband complained that after five years of marriage, his wife had gained weight, was unkept, lost her sense of fun and adventure, and spent most of her free time at her mother's house.

"This isn't the woman I married!" he fumed. "When we first got together she was passionate and affectionate. Now she treats me like I'm a rapist who climbed in through the bedroom window."

Many times the husband is directly responsible when a wife loses interest in herself and the marriage. It can be very frustrating for a woman if her husband stops communicating, gets wrapped up in his work or abuses her verbally or emotionally. On the other hand, there are women who pretend that they love sex and taking care of their man. These ladies should be sued for false advertising. Before marriage, they play the role of being hot, passionate women. They send a message that says. "This is just a sample of what you'll be getting if you marry me."

After the ceremony is over and the smoke clears, the truth begins to surface. This woman is not hot and passionate at all. It was just a performance to get what she wanted.

However, if you are a woman who has given marriage your absolute best, yet you are still going through a bad situation, don't allow the tough times to rob you of your beauty and self-esteem. Please remember that one of the greatest attributes of a woman who is full-of-beauty, is her ability to persevere. Before you give up or let yourself fall apart, get help! Pray without ceasing. Go to your pastor or a professional counselor. Be determined to make your marriage work.

Marriage is like a career move. You get an education so you can get a good job. When you get hired you don't say "I can relax now." Rather you work even harder, not only to keep your job, but because you want to make advancements. A good marriage with all the perks and advantages takes hard work.

A wise woman will learn how to live her life in seasons.

There is a season when she must give her full attention to being a loving and supportive wife. Her talents and energy will go into helping her mate establish himself in his career or business. It is important to build a solid financial base for the family with the husband establishing himself as a major contributor.

There is a season when she must give her attention to being a good mother. She must make sure her children develop their talents and gifts to the fullest. She must also help her children become disciplined, mature and obedient.

A woman who takes care of herself can live a long and productive life. As her children grow older and her husband settles into his work, there will be plenty of time left for her to "do her own thing," so to speak. I want to encourage you not to allow your job or career to rob your husband and children of the attention they need. Especially during the early years of your children's development. If at all possible, young children should spend the main part of their day with someone who loves them and is personally committed to their development. This should be a family member, like grandmom, auntie or someone who is very close to your family. Work at home or work at night if you have to, but do all in your power to make sure the gift of inner-beauty and self-esteem is passed on to your children by giving your family the time and attention they need.

There will come a season when a woman can say "This is my time to shine!" It's time for me to go back to school, build a business or a career. She may even desire to get involved in something that has been a long standing personal goal. Go for it! Enjoy it to the fullest.

I am not trying to paint you a picture of a house with a white picket fence, where your family lives happily ever after. We all know that there are times of great difficulties and times of great joy. There will be seasons when you will have to care for your parents. Seasons when your husband might lose his job, mess up the money or get involved with another woman. Only God can give a woman the grace and power to deal with the challenges of life, while still becoming more beauty-full as the years go by.

There is nothing more beauty-full than a couple who has weathered the storms of life together. In his eyes she is more beautiful with wrinkled hands and silver hair, then she ever was as a shapely young girl.

There are many women who have reached their 40's, 50's and 60's, who don't see themselves as attractive and desirable. Some of these women are often taken advantage of by some young Casanova who is after her house, car, credit cards and life savings. I'm not saying that an older woman should not fall in love with a sincere younger man. I am saying to be careful and prayerful and take council from the people who love you and are concerned about your welfare.

Age is no reason to let yourself go, or lose your sense of excitement and expectation. Watch your diet, get your exercise, dress in stylish clothes and stay active in your church and community. Let your beauty shine as you speak words of wisdom and encouragement to the people around you. Adopt sons and daughters. Most of all, look forward to meeting a man who wants to spend the second half of his life with a beauty-full woman just like you.

* * *

One of the most unforgettable stories in the Bible is a love story about the Song of Solomon and the Shulamite woman. The story was written by King Solomon using symbolic examples called metaphors. The story opens with a love-struck King who has discovered a beauty-full woman who's skin is dark "like the tents of Kedar" (a dark brown color). The King longs to bring the Shulamite into his palace and make her his bride. This creates a problem for the bride-to-be, because she does not feel worthy of the king's love. Her reasons for rejecting his love are recorded in the writings of Solomon.

*Song of Solomon 1:5: Don't despise me because
I am dark, the sun tanned me. My mother's sons
were angry with me. They made me keep their
vineyards, but my own vineyards I have not kept.*

It is hard to believe that over two thousand years ago, skin color was still an issue. Ladies of class and refinement did not work in the hot sun, therefore their complexions remained lighter. Darker skin was an indication that you were a common laborer and therefore poor. The Shulamite wears her color as a badge of shame, her words tell a story of low self-esteem and of a dysfunctional family that has obviously misused and abused her. Before meeting the king she was unkept, unwanted, unloved and unprepared for the better life that was now being offered to her.

She did not realize that the man who loved her, loved everything about her, including her hair, her eyes and the color of her skin. When a man truly loves a woman, everything about her is beauty-full. King Solomon's eyes could clearly see the beauty that had gone unrecognized all of her life.

Just as we have difficulty understanding why God loves us so much, and is ready and willing to accept us just as we are, the Shulamite could not understand the king's deep affection for her.

*Song of Solomon 6:13: (paraphrased) What
do you see in me, a Shulamite?*

King Solomon answers with a powerful affirmation of her beauty.

*Song of Solomon 7:1-9: (Paraphrased) How
beautiful are your feet. The curve of your thighs
are like jewels. Your navel is a rounded goblet.*

Your waist is a heap of wheat set about with lilies. Your breast are like two fawns. Your neck like an ivory tower. Your eyes like the pools of Hebron. Your nose is like the tower of Lebanon. Your hair is your crown. How fair and pleasant you are to look at.

God also delights in your creation. He loves the size and shape of your feet, legs, hips and waist. He also delights in your breasts, neck, face and hair. He wants you to see yourself through His eyes, and love and appreciate the way you were created, just as He loves and appreciates you. It is a wonder-full thing when you are in good health and able to walk with your legs, speak with your mouth, see with your eyes and hear with your ears.

Just as Solomon used words of truth to heal the Shulamite from a painful self-image, God uses the Word to heal us from a false perception of ourselves. Once we have been rejected or abused or done something that leaves us with feelings of guilt and shame, we think that God no longer sees us as acceptable and beauty-full. That is why Jesus came to renew our minds and to heal and cleanse us from all of our hurts and sins. He holds up a mirror that has no distortions in the glass. He shows us the real person. The one who is no longer a victim but a victor. The words ring out like a song of hope as Solomon continues in his quest to deliver his ebony queen from the bondage of self-hatred.

Song of Solomon 4:7 You are so beautiful my love there is no spot in you.

* * *

Beauty-full Women and their Sexuality

Whether a female is eight years old or eighty, if you study her behavior carefully, you will at some point witness a classic display of female sexuality. My little granddaughter has already mastered the art of smiling up at her daddy and in a soft cooing voice, she makes her request; "Daddy, I love you sooo much, pretty pleeease may I have a new doll baby."

Of course he melts with pride as he digs into his pocket to give his little ballerina the desires of her heart. It goes without saying that little Ashley learned the fine art of melting a man's heart, sitting at the feet of her mother.

Women can change the course of history with a carefully spoken word, or just the right look. No matter what presidential advisors have to say about the affairs of state, the woman lying next to the president has the final say.

Never let anyone make you believe that it is not of God for a woman's sensuality to make her man walk out of an important meeting just to be with her; spend his life savings on the house that she wants to live in; climb mountains and swim rivers, just for her amusement. From the first day that Adam set eyes on Eve, men have been inspired and driven by the quiet sensuality of women.

Contrary to the opinion of some, it doesn't take a

pound of makeup, a sexy dress, or imported perfume to drive a man up the wall. It may be a silly grin on a freshly washed face, or the way a silk blouse falls across her shoulder. After years of buying expensive clothes, wearing exotic hairdos and all the other trappings, I have come to the conclusion that for a real man, less is always more. What is understated makes the biggest statement. What is done out of innocence is the most unforgettable moment. It may be a gesture that was not meant for him that finds its way into his heart every time.

I asked several men what they considered sexy in a woman. The answers covered the gamut, but rarely touched on "see through" dresses and sexy underwear. Andrew smiled as he began to share with me how he met his wife. They were both counselors in a youth program. He watched her for months before they ever sat down and had a conversation.

"I really enjoyed watching her interact with the kids," he smiled. "They would do things to drive her crazy. She would put her hands on her hips and take a deep breath, trying not to lose her cool. A couple of times I came to her rescue, but she didn't even notice me. I loved her focus and dedication to what she was doing. On top of everything else, she was very sexy in a very nonchalant kind of way. Once I brought her a cup of water during a Volleyball match. She smiled at me, winked and said thank you. She didn't even notice, she wasn't even trying... but she was soooo sexy!"

Eric was hooked by a different set of events. He and Priscilla worked together. "One Saturday, Priscilla invited some of the people from her job to her house for a barbecue," he began. "Her grandmother opened the door. She gave me a big hug, like I was a long lost relative. Priscilla's mom was in the kitchen laughing and telling stories about the good old days. Her dad was in the backyard manning the grill. That man could make ribs stand up and holler. In the next few hours, I discovered the wildest, funniest, most loving people that I ever met. We played Dominoes, watched the baseball game on television and laughed all night. That's really how I fell in love with Priscilla. She wasn't the movie star type, but just like her family, she was so much fun to be with. She was funny, loving and her cooking really 'turned me on.' Priscilla came from a family of hard working people. She's very ambitious for both of us and can stretch a dollar from here to Texas. Not only did I marry a lady with a lot of sex appeal, but I married into the greatest family in the world."

Hank said that creative, imaginative, down-to-earth women were very sexy. Stan reported that a real turn on for him was an innocent little girl... "I need your protection" kind of lady. Another brother said he is fascinated by smart women who make you think you're smarter, even though you know you're not. One last anonymous brother said that he's like putty around ladies who know that they have the goods, yet they are approachable and sweet.

Sexuality is not always clingy clothes, soft music and lights. Be careful that you send a message of love and not lust. Men who are looking for lust are looking at what you have 'on your body.' Men who are looking for love, are looking at what you have 'in you heart.'

Remember, love sends out a message of commitment and trust. Lust sends out a message of no commitment and let's keep it short and sweet.

While a woman's sexuality was never intended to be used as a trap to catch men, it is still the lure that keeps a potential suitor circling overhead. And it's still the force that will make a man work hard to build his kingdom so he can lay it at her feet. It will also cause a man to pass up a chance to hang out with the fella's and head straight home to you.

Unfortunately, women no longer seem to understand what real sensuality is all about. Too many have bought into a false and superficial concept of sexuality. Real sexuality is the quiet fire that emanates from the spirit within a woman which makes her the attractive woman that she was meant to be.

Once again, I must remind you that the beauty of a woman comes from the inside. A woman can be younger, older or bigger and still be beauty-full. The "X" factor that drives a man wild emanates from all types of women. It has nothing to do with the her weight, skin color or the texture of her hair. Like an invisible force, the beauty on the inside draws men like bees looking for honey and bankers searching for money. Since men are attracted visually first, physical attributes do have their advantages. But it's all about what a woman does with the attributes that she has that makes the difference. A woman should do all in her power to decorate her exterior and make herself a lovely sight to behold. Remember, whatever is in a woman's heart, will be reflected in her attire. Whether she is casual or dressed in her best, her clothing should say that she is full of love, wisdom, peace, joy and all the other fruits of the spirit.

Colors and styles should be worn with confidence. Every woman should learn how to 'strut her stuff' in a very classy way. Don't be hung up on your skin color or your size. Black women were made for bright tropical colors. If you are a woman and you love being a woman, then flaunt your femininity. On special occasions, step out of the hip-hop gear, dump the suit and briefcase and let the real woman take center stage. Try wearing a lovely hat, a flowing silk dress, with a matching jacket or coat and a pair of sexy high heels. Hats and high heels tend to make women hold their heads higher and walk with more elegance. Soft feminine clothes drive men wild. Men feel more like men when a woman's hair smells like jasmine, her earrings sparkle and her nails are manicured.

When it comes to your face, there is no cosmetic line that works better than the glow that comes from the love of

God. Wisdom and joy make a woman's lips appealing. Especially when she adds just the right touch of mango or raspberry coloring. Her words ring out, bringing laughter and brightness, attracting people to her. It makes her husband love to hear her voice. It comforts her children and encourages her friends.

The sexiest eyes in the world can be found in a woman who is honest, trustworthy and full of faith. Her eyes are always clear and bright. You can almost look into her soul. Again bronze, gold, or soft aqua blue will only give more illumination to the light that radiates from you. A man should be able to look directly into your eyes without feeling uneasy and fearful. When he looks at you, he can speak his heart and share his dreams without feeling intimidated.

A perfect nose belongs to a woman who keeps it out of other people's business and to the grindstone. If your nose is oily, a little translucent powder should make you picture perfect. Your nose should be able to smell trouble and take a detour. It is important that a beauty-full woman keep her environment peaceful and trouble-free. Her man should be able to smell the perfume of her confidentiality and integrity as he opens up and lets her into his soul.

Your hands are power-full, yet carefully manicured. They should always be open to give of yourself and be helpful and full of good works.

When there is no man in your life to share your love with, pour your heart to the people around you who are in need of love and attention. *Remember, love gives - lust takes.* Be a play-mother or a sister to a lonely young person. A daughter and a friend to your elders. As that special man watches you "give" and pour out your affection on others, his desire for you will begin to surface. While you are waiting for Mr. Right, you can keep loneliness and frustration from setting in by giving your love to those who desperately need your affection and attention. I am a living witness that, in return, you will be rewarded with love, appreciation, and the peace that passes all understanding. When you put your life in His divine hands, you won't have a lot of time left to feel lonely and frustrated.

Above all, remember that "old" women are never attractive. No matter what your age, you don't have to be "old." Be involved, energetic, up to date and in the mix! We will all die some day. Please don't fizzle out. Go out with a bang!

* * *

If you have been blessed with a loving husband, or you hope to be married someday, just remember that men are like cars: If they are properly serviced on a regular basis and treated with care, you'll get a lot of mileage out of your man.

Men love the smell of French perfume, but they also love the smell of baked bread and smothered chicken. Don't be tricked into believing that a liberated woman doesn't belong in the kitchen. Home cooked meals are the fellowship that keeps couples together. Try spending an evening with you and your man fixing a meal together. Let him chop while you saute. Do a lot of hugging and kissing in between. Sexy cooking and sexual intimacy will make a man forever sing your praises.

When you are not being intimate with your man in the kitchen, be the jewel in his crown by becoming the "hostess with the mostest." Learn how to entertain his friends and business associates with a flair that is uniquely "you." Make all the other men wish for a woman like you. Your man's chest will be stuck out with pride when you make him look good with a gourmet meal, candlelights, flowers, and whatever unique and sexy things you've stored up for special occasions.

A woman who's playing for keeps will become a master in the kitchen as well as the bedroom. Why not take a short course in massage therapy. Drive his tired body crazy by knowing just where a special touch is needed. In turn, help him learn how to "do you," when you need to relax. Buy some nice scented oils and candles... and don't tell yourself you've been together too long to play house... use them!

While you're making the man in your life relax and feel better, be sure to talk to him in a soft voice, using words that affirm him. Whisper to him that he is your champion. Talk about the great things you are going to do together. Tell him how much you appreciate him. Be specific about the nice things he does for you. If you can't think of any, then think again. The more you say good things about him, the more he will gradually do all in his power to become the man that you are describing.

I was really impressed with Eddie Murphy's wife during a recent appearance on the Oprah Winfrey show. Oprah asked her what she liked most about Eddie. Instead of talking about how funny he is, how rich, or how large she was living, she took another route that made Eddie blush with pride.

"First of all, he is an excellent and very involved father to his children. Most people think of Eddie as a guy who is very funny," she continued. "But the thing that constantly amazes me, is how brilliant he is. He is a great thinker and a very clever businessman. I know that whatever he does concerning our family or in business, he has thought it through very carefully."

She applauded him for things that really mattered. Her words stayed with me because of her sincerity in expressing her appreciation for having such a wonder-full man in her life. If she was acting, then I take my hat off to her.

Many African-American women are in dire need of tongue taming lessons, particularly when dealing with men. I encourage my sisters not to be loud and bossy, loud and negative, or loud and critical, especially with the man that matters most to you. If things are not going well, pray, count to ten, take a walk, or clean your closet before speaking. Put your feelings in check and deal with the real issues. Try to be positive and constructive as you "discuss," not fight over the issues that you are trying to resolve. If you're tired of the same old stuff then get help, but don't reduce yourself to a nagging, raving maniac. No matter what you think, or what your momma did, verbal lashings don't work very well with men. Save them for your children and your pets.

If you want your husband to be good to you, then don't ever forget to tell him how much you appreciate him. If our heavenly Father likes to hear us praise Him, then it will certainly work on the man that God gave you.

And always, whether you are single or married, be beautiful and sexy when you go to bed at night. Get rid of the "T" shirts, please! Take a trip to Victoria Secrets. This is not a treat, it is an investment in you and your future. Fix your bedroom and bathroom up first! Use big soft pillows, cozy quilts, soft colors, pretty sheets and relaxing art on the walls. The bathroom should be full of shower gels, scented lotions, oils, a massage shower head, and lots of good smelling stuff to dump in your bath water so you and yours can relax. Let your bedroom reflect that you are a sensual, warm and cuddly woman.

One of the best kept secrets that most women have yet to learn is that there is a direct correlation between the way a woman worships God and her capacity for sexual intimacy. Many women pretend to be involved in worship, but it is simply that... a pretense. Other women are too shallow or inhibited to openly show love for God. But there are women who are so intimate with the living God that they cannot restrain themselves when they are in the presence of the Holy Spirit.

Women who love God deeply may stand quietly weeping, but you can feel their intensity as they whisper words of praise and thanksgiving. Other women move into wild abandonment. They dance, sway, laugh, yell, and jump. They are more excited than the biggest fan cheering for the home team. Perhaps you are still wondering what worship and praise has to do with sexual intimacy.

A single woman should learn to refrain from promiscuous relationships, and at the same time, release her spirit to be intimate with God in worship. Once she is married, her body will beautifully express to her husband what her spirit has learned from intimacy with God.

The joy of sex is not in how many positions a woman knows, but in the power and intensity that is released from her spirit when she is in the arms of her man.

A woman who indulges in multiple relationships before marriage will stretch, damage and disease her female organs and dull her appetite for sexual intimacy. Her spirit does not know how to reach out and embrace her husband's spirit because she never learned how to be intimate with God. The residue of her past lovers is still creating a barrier. She will also have problems if she has never learned how to be intimate with God.

A married woman must be careful not to lose her appetite and interest in sex. All too often, women use sex as a way to reward men for good deeds or good behavior. A night on the town, a new car, or fixing the roof could mean a sexual treat. "Performance based sex" is nothing more than a subtle form of prostitution. Sexual intimacy should always be based on an expression of genuine affection and a natural desire of intimacy. Believe it or not, a woman can keep her sexual edge, by working on her intimacy with God. On numerous occasions, I have known men who have sent their wives on spiritual retreats, only to have the best sex ever upon their return. The reason is profound, yet simple.

There is no way that a couple can live together without experiencing disappointments, disagreement and differences. Unfortunately, many of these thoughts and feelings go unresolved. The "buildup" creates a silent barrier. The first place this barrier may be felt is in their communication. Feelings go unexpressed and if words are exchanged, instead of clarity, they lead to more misunderstandings. The next barrier to be erected is in the bedroom. The man desires to satisfy his sexual urge, regardless of the problems. The woman, on the other hand, becomes closed emotionally and sexually.

A time of prayer, fasting, and worship before the Lord will wash away the build up in the husband and the wife. The offenses and disagreements quickly dissolve as the woman embraces the Lord in praise, worship and adoration. Once she is open to spiritual intimacy, physical intimacy will follow its natural course.

Another road block to sexual intimacy is "overload." Too much pressure and too little rest can quickly put sex on the bottom of the priority list, if not off the list all together. If you don't have time or you're too tired to be loved by your man, than it's time to look at your priorities and reorder your life before it's too late.

First stop and remember why you got married in the first place. Hopefully, you married so you could be together as much as possible. As you said "I do," you were looking forward to the time when you could make love 'til the cows came home.' It didn't matter if you were in a palace or a one room apartment. It didn't matter if you had more 'bills than money,' or if you had a million dollars in the bank. Just being in touching distance of each other was always the bottom line. But when the babies start to come and the bills pile up, and the work-load includes: dropping off the kids, going to work, stopping at the grocery store, cooking dinner, helping with homework... did you say "sex...?" as in, missing sleep? Exerting more energy? Whispering sweet nothings?

Only a superwoman can keep this kind of schedule

without coming apart at the seams. Don't be afraid to reorder your life. If you are too busy for your man, you are too busy. Here are some suggestions that you can think about that will give you more time together:

1. Find a family member or pay someone to help you with your children.
2. Look into starting a "home-based business." If you are good with computers, baking, or accounting, think about working out of your home. If done correctly, you should have more time to rest and be ready for your family at the end of the day.
3. Become a consultant, or work part-time, rather than full time employment.
4. If possible, choose a simpler life-style that allows you to stay at home. You may not have a lot of money, but it will do wonders for your marriage.
5. Start a neighborhood co-op that shares in baby-sitting, picking up and dropping off kids and other draining responsibilities.
6. Learn to check into a hotel with your mate for a night, even if it's around the corner from your house.
7. Take a long lunch with your husband or check into a hotel for an afternoon together.

Relationships go through many stages. Some of the stages are more enjoyable than others. Hopefully, as we look at the different stages of a relationship, it will help you stay on track.

ATTRACTION: This is the first stage of a relationship. When you meet that special someone, your heart beats fast, your hands get sweaty and your words become jumbled. Sexual feelings are at a high pitch and can easily get you into trouble. It is only natural that you would want this euphoric feeling to last forever. But the rush of adrenaline at the sound of his voice will soon diminish. Many people who are not mature will take this as a sign that the "thrill is gone." In reality, the high that you experience when you first meet should give way to the next phase of the relationship.

BONDING: This is the time when things begin to quiet down a bit, but the feelings should still remain strong. This is a time of getting to know the "real person." The 90% that is living beneath the skin. This period will expose personality, character, special gifts, plans, and dreams. Most of all, you will discover areas where you are compatible and incompatible. If the two of you decide to take the plunge, you must first go through a "rubbing" before the bonding is completed. Please get some good advice and counseling before you sign on the dotted line. Marriage is one of the most important decisions that you will ever make. "Only fools rush in where angels fear to tread."

In the bonding process you will get on each other's nerves. You will have to give up things and put up with things that go against the fantasy of how you thought it would be. But if the love between you is strong and true, you will make it through the process of becoming one flesh.

BUILDING: If you make it through the first two phases, then and only then will the real purpose of your relationship unfold. Remember the commandment: "Be fruitful, multiply, subdue the earth and have dominion over it." More than any other phase of your relationship, the beauty that is on the inside of a woman will begin to surface. To build, she must be strong, even if her appearance is fragile. She must be a hard worker, she must have faith, and be an encourager. She must be a team player and be able to endure disappointments and failures. She must know how to pray her way into her desired goals.

ROLE MODELS: Counselors may understand the principles of a success-full relationship, but it takes a couple who has prayed together and stayed together to model the real and lasting power of love. Years ago, young couples could turn to their parents and other family members for advice on how to build a strong and lasting relationship. But with the deterioration of families, and the soaring divorce rate, it is difficult to find couples who can serve as role models for success-full and fruit-full relationships. Nothing sends a stronger message of unity and strength than a couple who has been together for years and still demonstrate love and affection toward one another.

CELEBRATION: If you work together and do a lot of forgetting and forgiving, you should be looking forward to a time of enjoyment and renewed sexual pleasure. The kids should be doing their own thing, the finances should be stabilizing, and most of your dreams should be realized. With good health, the bills paid, and the babies out of the way, sex should be more enjoyable than ever. It's time for cruises, vacations, camping trips and anniversary celebrations. If you're going through a difficult stage with your husband, do all in your power to hang in there. Remember, 70% of all divorces are initiated by women. If God could change you, then believe that he will do the same for your mate. What he's going through may just be one of the many stages that we will all pass through sooner or later.

* * *

Sexual intimacy also has another deadly enemy of which women should be fully aware. Diseases that are connected to diet can cause sexual impotency in men in general and Black men in particular. Diabetes and high blood pressure and heart disease are three of the main culprits. In the Old Testament, God did not allow the Children of Israel to eat swine. God called this animal unclean. This means that the meat was poisonous to mankind.

During slavery, we were forced to eat swine to survive. We developed a taste for the most poisonous part of the pig, the intestines, better known as "chitterlings." In celebration of our heritage and on special occasions, African Americans continue to eat Mr. Swine's ears, snout, tail, feet, testicles and intestines. On a more regular basis, African American's eat 'higher on the hog.' Ham, bacon and smothered pork chops and peach cobbler (loaded with butter and sugar) are the silent robbers of male sexual potency, as well as their lives. As soon as an African-American male finds out he has high blood pressure, the first thing the doctor tells him is to stop eating pork and to watch his salt, starch and sugar intake. Since Black men have the highest rate of high blood pressure of all racial groups in America, why not take preventive measures by removing pork, sugar, salt, and starch out of your diet and his diet.

Poor diet and eating habits can also lead to diabetes and heart disease. Diabetes keeps the body from properly processing starchy foods and sugar. High doses of sugar in food add to the problem. The result can lead to blindness, lack of energy, infections and weight gain. It also causes constriction of the blood vessels, which blocks the flow of blood. This makes erection difficult, and sometimes impossible, for men suffering from this disease.

High blood pressure and heart disease do not necessarily cause impotency. But many of the medications that are used to control the disease, interrupt sexual performance in males. Some men would rather risk having a stroke or heart attack than be deprived of sex.

A wise woman will start early, while her man is still

young and healthy to prepare high fiber, low fat meals that will protect her man's health as well as his sexual performance. If he smokes, drinks or uses drugs (even if he calls himself a "social" drinker or drug user), do all in your power to help him quit. What he calls a social life-style or a controlled habit, will quickly become out of control if, and when, a crisis should arise in his life. Help him learn how to relax in prayer, exercise, sports and good entertainment.

Fasting is a good way to break bad habits and to bring your beauty-full body under control. Prepare mentally first. Let your body know what will be happening in the next few days. When you feel you are ready to go without food, first take a cleansing enema or a good natural laxative. If you have never fasted before, pick up a book on fasting from a health store or a Christian book store. Start with a short fast. Go from sun up to sun down with spring water, and a twist of lemon if you choose. A teaspoon of honey may be added if you need energy for your work day. Break the fast with fruit, salad or soup. Next, set a day aside for a twenty four hour fast. Try to do it on your day off. Be sure to cleanse your bowels first. Then begin with spring water or distilled water, with lemon and honey if needed.

Of course there are many ways to fast. I strongly advise that you have some sort of fasting program for you and your mate so you can live a healthy and beauty-full life together.

* * *

All too often I talk to women who do not enjoy sex and dislike having sex all together. Needless to say, this attitude can create a great deal of problems in the bedroom. Some men are just not good lovers. If this is the case, get to the bottom of the problem with the help of a trained therapist. If you find sex painful or very uncomfortable, you should see a doctor immediately. Unfortunately, for some women, disliking sex goes deeper than having an inadequate partner or a health problem. In many cases it can be traced back to sexual abuse at an early age. I have wept with women who were molested by their fathers, grandfathers, brothers or teachers. The memories of these violations can leave deep mental, emotional and spiritual scars.

For many women, it isn't until they are grown and experience sexual intimacy that the memories of sexual abuse begin to surface. Some women unconsciously choose a partner who has many traits of her past abuser. The results can be devastating. The man that she sleeps with doesn't understand what he is doing wrong or why she is rejecting him. Because of her mental and emotional confusion, she may not realize what is happening but still acts out her anger and frustrations. To make matters worse, she may be too ashamed and hurt to deal with the awful truth. If she and her husband do not get help, the relationship will continue to deteriorate and the internal turmoil can reach an explosive level. She may become an abusive parent, engage in destructive behavior, or destroy her own marriage to be free from her husband and the pain of intimacy.

The good news is, I have seen hundreds and thousands of women set free from sexual violations which held them in bondage for years. I know that there is life after abuse, because I am a survivor.

Once a woman has been wounded and has lived with the pain and crippling effects of abuse, the hardest thing to do is open up and let the wound be exposed in order to heal. It may cause family disputes and painful upheavals. However, the questions that you must ask yourself are: Can you continue to live with the pain? Are you willing to jeopardize your future, your marriage, or your mental well being to keep your secret safe?

No matter how hard you try, eventually the pain and rage will surface. It will find a way to express itself in a way that you will have no control over. It will manifest in a nervous breakdown, a chronic illness, or behavior of which you never realized you were capable. Trust and believe me when I tell you that the best way to deal with the pain of the past is to find a counselor or a confidante. Let it out while you are still in control of your actions. Ask God for the strength to deal with it. He will never leave you and never forsake you.

In order for your sexuality to flourish you must maintain good spiritual health, mental health, emotional health and physical health. Take care of the "whole" you. Check your breast for lumps. If you are over forty, *get a mammogram*, which is an x-ray that checks the breasts for cancer. Make sure that you get an annual *pap smear*, which is a vaginal exam that checks for cancer.

Don't sleep around! It is both mentally and physically destructive. HIV and AIDS are higher among Black women than any other racial group. There will be times during the month when your hormones will make your body scream for sex. These difficult periods will pass. AIDS however, is forever! It is the most horrible curse ever known to mankind. It is a culmination and assortment of diseases emerging on the same body in a relentless attack. You may experience tuberculoses, pneumonia, hepatitis and a variety of infections that cannot be controlled.

If you are married and there is strong evidence that your husband is unfaithful, *don't tolerate adultery.* Bring his gravy train to a screeching halt until you are able to resolve the problem. "Strong evidence" is not what your momma heard on the street, or what your girlfriend tried to tell you. You must have personal knowledge before you take action. With the rise of intravenous drug use, multiple partners, and bisexual practices, sexual infidelity in marriage should not be taken lightly.

Sex was meant to be a beauty-full experience, but whenever a gift is abused, we forfeit the pleasure that it was intended to bring.

We bring the joy back into sex when we honor the boundaries that are designed to bring maximum pleasure and fulfillment.

In order for a man to treat you with respect and value you as a woman, you must first value and respect yourself. Whether you are married or single, you must establish boundaries in the relationship that must never be violated. If you have a "do me right - do me wrong - but just do me!" attitude, that is exactly what a man will eventually do. He will "do you in!" Let him know from the beginning that God is good to you and you are good to yourself, therefore you expect comparable treatment from him. By establishing personal boundaries, you allow the beauty inside of you to continue to flourish. It also keeps us from damaging the beauty of the people we love.

My mother and father were married for almost fifty years and in all those years, there were certain things that were not acceptable in their relationship. My mother made it clear that she did not want my father to discuss their problems with people outside of the family. Once when he cursed at her, I'm not sure what happened, but when I walked into the room, he was picking himself up off the floor. He had crossed a boundary and had to deal with the consequences.

By the same token, my father had rules and boundaries for how my mother should behave in relationship with him. He expected his food to be put aside if he wasn't around for dinner. My mother always made a big fuss about keeping dad's food ready for him. He expected my mother to always consult him before making a major purchase. I can still remember him leaning up against our refrigerator, not realizing it was brand new. We sat at the kitchen table holding our breaths. In a few minutes, the fireworks started.

You may be viewed as arrogant or controlling for taking a stand with the man in your life, but establish and stick to the boundaries that you have set. In other words, protect yourself. "You" are all that you really have.

Boundary number one: Never compromise your relationship with God for the sake of a man. If he wants you to participate in something that is against your spiritual beliefs, you have every right to say no!

Boundary number two: Never let a man misuse your body. Just because you are married, it does not give him the right to force you to be involved in a practice that is repulsive to you.

Boundary number three: Never throw away your personal goals and ambitions, or stop thinking for yourself. You are not a robot. You are not a slave or a doormat. You are a talented, gifted and purposeful woman. Never lose sight of who God intended you to be.

Boundary number four: Never let a man threaten or abuse you verbally, mentally or spiritually. Not in public or in private. The "B" word should never be tolerated. And please, whatever you do, don't act like one.

You are too beauty-full to violate yourself by acting ugly. Most of all, you are too beauty-full to allow anyone else to violate you. There are other ways to deal with difficult situations. Once you sacrifice your personal identity, or allow yourself to be devalued in any way, it will be hard to reclaim what you have lost.

It is my earnest prayer that every woman find sexual fulfillment. I pray that you have a man in your life who looks at you with loving eyes. If not a husband, then someone who really cares about you and is there for you. I pray that if it is your desire, you will experience the joy of feeling your baby move inside of you for the first time. I pray that the child will know his father and that the father will be a faithful husband to you. I pray, that every single woman with children will be blessed with a man who will love her and her children. I pray that you will never be lonely. I pray that the man that God gives you will survive the attacks that will come against him and his family.

It is my earnest prayer that every woman who has suffered a broken heart will find healing at the foot of the cross. I pray that women will not compete with one another but comfort and affirm one another.

If we are to survive, we must constantly and continually pray for one another.

* * *

Wrestling with my Sister

Bunny Wilson sat in a chair across from me looking cool and indifferent. My arms were folded tightly across my chest as John Staggers, a man that Bunny and I greatly respected, looked at us both. He groaned softly before he spoke.

Little did we know that John was rapidly moving toward the end of his life. In retrospect, I now realize that he was giving those people who were near and dear to him a very precious gift. He shared with each of us what he believed the future held for our lives.

"God has a great work for you and for Bunny," he said in his mysterious tone. "You and Bunny must learn to love one another and walk together."

I should have hired a photographer to take a picture of my face as he finished the sentence. I can tell you that only in my worst nightmare could I imagine doing anything with Bunny Wilson. Across the room Bunny stared blankly at John. She showed no emotion, but I could read her thoughts. "Work with Terri McFaddin? Not in this life."

For the next few years, John Staggers' prediction proved to be false... wrong! Never... ever... could Bunny and I be friends, let alone sisters, let alone co-warriors fighting against every evil work that was holding women hostage around the world.

Unfortunately for us both, I worked with Bunny's husband, Frank Wilson. Our children were friends. We attended the same church and shared the same friends. But we argued about everything. Our criticisms of one another were relentless. I complained about her and she complained about me. Things were so bad between us that it finally led to a showdown.

Frank was out of town on the night that Bunny called me on the telephone. She was not her usual cool, calm and always "in control" self. She was livid.

"This has got to stop! I have had just about enough! We need to talk!"

"I'll be right over!" I replied. "I've got a few things to settle with you too!" I said, slamming the telephone down.

I jumped in my car and headed for her house with smoke coming out of my ears. But as I drove through the streets, the Spirit of the Lord began to speak to me.

"At some point you're going to have to listen to someone and hear what needs to be said about you, and to you. If you listen to Bunny and if you stop hating her so much, she can help you grow."

I was so angry, I wanted to scream. It was true. I had been in control of my own life for many years. There was no one in my life to criticize or dispute my decisions. No one to tell me how to improve and grow into the woman that God really wanted me to be. No one except Bunny Wilson.

"Lord you have a real sense of humor," I thought to myself.

I thought about Juanita Scott. We had been friends for at least twenty years. She was my serious "homegirl." We did good things together and we did bad things together. Bunny was a stickler for being on time and doing things according to the plan. Juanita and I were always late, and always coming up with a new plan. It drove Bunny crazy and we both knew it.

On the weekends, Juanita and I used to sneak out to the clubs on the other side of town away from the church members. We would meet guys and dance the night away. Juanita and I both loved God, but we loved being silly too. But now God was calling us to put away childish things, and Bunny Wilson was the thorn in my side who was always demanding that I set a higher standard for moral and spiritual excellence.

Juanita made no such demands. She accepted me for who I was and where I was. We were "homeys," shopping buddies. Whenever we got together, our goal was to play, eat and shop til we dropped.

My thought returned to my upcoming meeting. Something inside of me wanted to do the right thing. By the time I arrived at Bunny's house, I was ready and willing to listen to her criticisms, and if they were legitimate, I was willing to make changes.

Bunny's face was like stone as the two of us sat in Frank's office. She pulled out a list that she had prepared earlier. She wanted to make sure that she didn't miss any of the offenses and problems that she was having with me.

"Number one," her voice was trembling as she spoke. "You have no regard for time or the appointments that you make with me. You were an hour late the last time we met for lunch and you didn't even bother to apologize or make an excuse."

She paused for a moment waiting for me to counter about something she had done wrong, or to find an excuse for my actions.

"I was wrong," I said. "I'm very sorry that I disrespected you. Please forgive me."

Bunny stared at me as if she was waiting for the punch line. But there was none. After a long silence, she read her second grievance. "I don't appreciate you gossiping with people about things that I asked you to keep confidential."

I thought about what she was saying. I thought about conversations with Carolyn Caston, Gwen Brown and some other mutual "friends."

"Yes, I did say such and such," I confessed. "I am really sorry that I hurt you, it won't happen again."

By the time Bunny got half way down the list, we were both crying. She crumbled the paper and began to confess to me things that she had done wrong. She asked my forgiveness. In the middle of the conversation there was a power failure in the house. Bunny played with the switch, but the circuit was dead. We sat in the dark talking. She shared her deepest fears. The pain of being rejected by her mother.

"If I was one minute late coming out of school, my mother would drive off and I'd have to make that long walk home alone. That's why when you're late, I take it personally. It brings back painful memories," she explained.

I sat in the dark sharing painful secrets with Bunny that I have never told anyone. We cried, we hugged, we forgave. When we walked out of the room, we realized that what we thought was a blackout had only happened in Frank's study. Except for the room that we were in, the lights were still on all over the house.

Sometimes God has to blind women to the exterior and superficial things, so we can see into one another's souls. It goes without saying that we were both called into the ministry. Bunny has authored four books and has traveled around the world. And of course, I'm doing my thing too. We still have disagreements from time to time. We both can be extremely sensitive, but I do love and respect Bunny Wilson with all of my heart.

Every woman should have a sister in her life who pushes her toward excellence. Someone who has paid the price to make constructive criticisms about your personal and public life. The relationship requires you to be mature enough to take the heat if your sister takes a bite out of you, because she's not ready to hear the truth. If you are really family, she'll not only get over it, but she will thank you in the end for caring enough to tell her the truth.

The most important thing that I have learned from my twenty + years relationship with Bunny is that women should really pay attention to women who they seem to be at odds with. *The truth is that if certain women ever really hookup, the power between them can shake the earth.* That is why there can be tremendous tension and feelings of competition between women who may not even know how power-full and gifted they are. Sometimes the eyes of a woman can see the potential in her sister more clearly than the sister in question sees herself.

It was only when Bunny and I put our differences aside and began to focus on our common goals, that God was able to use us both effectively.

The barriers that separate women are without question straight out of the pit of hell. We need each other and we know we need each other. Yet, we are forever getting tangled up in personalities, petty issues, real and imagined offenses, age, color, size and shape. All are designed to keep us struggling to get to the top, only to land right back into the bottom of the barrel.

I thank God for the lessons that I have learned on my journey through sisterhood. I have noticed that the younger generation of women seem to be less willing to forget and forgive. They claim to have "associates," instead of sister-friends. I believe that it is up to the women who are in a place of emotional and spiritual maturity to encourage younger sisters to hang-in-there with each other. It is important that they challenge one another to be excellent in their quest to become women who are full-of-beauty and beauty-full. We must first set the example by hanging in there ourselves.

Even through all the struggles, I am so glad that many of the sisters that I started out with are still in my life. Each one of them taught me a valuable lesson. In one way or another, they helped me get to the next level. The one's who stayed on track, have done very well in life. Whenever we get together, we sit down and talk about the petty fights and the terrible things we did to one another as a result of our spiritual immaturity. But if you hang in there, things will change, people will grow up.

It was Juanita Scott who taught me about forgetting and forgiving. I was dating a man who I was very much in love with. Through a series of events, I discovered that Juanita and another sister were secretly doing things to hinder my relationship with this wonderful man. When I confronted her with the evidence, after she got over the shock, she sincerely admitted that she was wrong and asked my forgiveness. She was like a child, caught with her hand in the cookie jar. She didn't make any excuses or try to pass the blame on to someone else. She simply asked my forgiveness.

"I forgive you," I fumed. "But just stay away from me! I never want to see your face again," I said slamming down the phone.

She called me back a hundred times, but I refused to talk with her. The next night, I had a quiet dinner party for my boyfriend and a few other people. Guess who showed up and sat down at the table like nothing was wrong? I stared at Juanita in disbelief.

"I love you and I'm sorry," she said, reaching for the plate of chicken. "Just because I made a mistake, you can't just throw me away. After all, I'm your daughter's godmother." Of course at that point, little Theresa climbed into her lap and hugged her neck. The people at the table stared at her, then back at me. She wasn't embarrassed, fearful or ashamed. She just refused to go away. Fifteen years have gone by. Now, instead of getting angry, we laugh together about what happened. When you get angry and try to throw your sister away, you will only have to go through a different set of changes with a different kind of woman. It is important to go "through" the changes with our sisters. Bailing out when things get difficult keeps us emotionally weak, immature and unable to deal with the stress of conflict. Conflict teaches us about the frailties of being human. We learn how to harness our pride, exercise self-control, forget, forgive and go on to the next thing.

Unresolved conflicts leave behind a trail of broken relationships, bitterness, and unforgiveness that keeps you living in the past. Sisters like Juanita will always be beauty-full in my eyes because she taught me by example how to make a mistake, apologize and go on together.

Another significant group of women in my life are the nine sisters that I have been meeting with for the last ten years. We decided that if we really wanted to become effective servants to African American people, we needed to come together once a year for a time of prayer, fasting, healing and encouragement. These sisters made Bunny Wilson look like an amateur when it came to challenging me to become a woman of excellence.

Whether your sisters come from blood relationships, spiritual relationships or extended family, they are God's plan for adding beauty to our lives. A true sister-friend is the best mirror for seeing a true reflection of yourself and knowing what you're really all about. She's always around to help you with the right hairdos, give you the latest fashions tips, help you with your networking, and problem solving. She's there to help you get through the hard times and celebrate life. Her love and concern is like a sweet melody playing on the car radio. Most of the time you are not really paying attention, you take the music for granted while its playing, but you really miss it when its not around. The words usually sound like this:

"Girl, is my skirt too tight? Should I put a jacket on?... Tomorrow, I'm picking you up at 6:00am sharp! We have got to get back on our exercise program... Ask your husband if he knows a good mechanic who can fix my car for a better price than that guy I've been using... If you want me to watch the kids this weekend be sure to pack some warm clothes, I might take them hiking in Big Bear park... Can I borrow your black jacket? I need it for a special meeting."

I can't think about borrowing stuff without thinking about my two blood sisters. Marlene Daniels and Lillian Jones. Looking back on how we grew up, makes me realize that those years laid the foundation for how I would treat all other women.

I am the oldest sibling in the family. When my mother and father were not at home, I was in charge. Even now, for better or for worse, I am still ready to take charge of meetings, decide what movie we are going to see, how to get from point "A" to point "B," and all other matters great and small. I still act like the oldest child in every situation. I am always protective of young children and people who are weak or needy. I'm good at settling disputes. I'm good at handling emergencies. I can always figure out how to make things happen. Last, but not least, I don't get upset when people borrow my stuff and don't return it. Developing good relationships takes a thick skin and real perseverance. Having two sisters certainly helped to develop my people skills.

My sister Marlene had a harder row to hoe. She wasn't the oldest, she wasn't the youngest, she wasn't the only girl. She was the infamous "middle child." She was strong-willed and noisy. You always knew when she was in the house because of all the noise. She was the smartest, the most ambitious; took more risk and got more beatings than anyone in the house. I guess that's why she's so successful today. By the same token she was loyal, funny and would give you the shirt off her back. She was fiercely protective of our baby sister Lil.

If anybody messed with Lil, you would have to deal with Marlene. And it has remained that way to this very day. Having Marlene for a friend is the best thing that could happen to a sister. Through the years, she has come to my rescue on more occasions than I can remember. She is truly my sister and friend.

Lillian, my youngest sister faced her own set of challenges. Not only was she the baby of the family, but unlike her two older sisters who have light brown complexions. Lil has a darker, reddish brown coloring. As I look back at the unkind names we called each other as it related to the color of our skin, it's a miracle that we even speak to each other at all. Thank God for a mother who made us feel beautiful and loved, no matter what the color of our skin, or what our hair looked like. While Marlene and I were very adventurous, Lil was a homebody. She was always following mom around, while Mar and I were looking for ways to escape. Lillian could clean a house like it was about to be inspected by the Board of Health. She always followed the rules. And if it hadn't been for Marlene, she would have never gotten into trouble.

When Marlene and I took her with us to see the Motown review at the Uptown Theater, it was sold out when we got there. I just had to see Smoky Robinson and the Miracles, so Mar and I came up with a plan to sneak by the usher who was watching the door. Our only problem was that Lil was with us. She was the baby. She was scared, and she didn't know how to lie. Marlene distracted the doorman while I sneaked by. I signaled for Lil, but she froze in her tracks. I don't know why the man didn't see me when I snatched Lil by her sweater and dragged her into the theater. On the surface, Lillian is fragile and not as assertive, but I have learned over the years, that when things get tough, she is the one you can always count on to make good decisions in the face of adversity. I guess we all got some of our mother's strength.

When our mother was diagnosed with cancer, everyone thought that Lillian would fall apart because she was the youngest and the closest to my mother. But to everyone's surprise, I was the one who collapsed when I heard the news. I literally fainted. I was so shaken, it was days before I could pull myself together and go to see her. It was Lil who kept Marlene, myself and the rest of the family as well, from falling completely apart.

I later learned that my mother had confided in Lil. "Watch over your big sister, I think she's going to take losing me very hard."

I have friends who, like my sister Lil, seem fragile and not very assertive. But in tough times they came to my rescue. I had strong, assertive friends, who ran for cover when the going got too tough. Having sisters has helped me to understand the complexities of dealing with women.

Like all people, we are the products of our backgrounds. When I am dealing with people in business or in social settings, the way they were raised will always surface. When I am with a woman who grew up as an only child, I can see the traces of a person who is not only use to getting her way, but is use to getting her share of attention. She sometimes finds it difficult to share her possessions with others. Her strong points are that she is usually self motivated and knows how to take care of herself. The woman who is the baby of her family is waiting for her instructions and will go along with any program that is reasonable. She has a tendency to be fiercely loyal to family and friends. She looks up to successful women and works hard to emulate their strengths.

The woman who grew up as a middle child is usually the rebel. She feels she has something to prove. She will probably be the one to start her own company, get involved in politics and live a very flamboyant life-style.

A women who is the oldest child is always prepared

to take the lead. They make good presidents and committee chairpersons. Their shortcomings are that they can be bossy, controlling and manipulative.

My best friend in high school was Sandy Duncan. She was an only child. She was a strong willed, survivor type who knew how to take care of herself. She had temper tantrums when she didn't get her way, but they never lasted long. She loved to come to my house because of all the people and all the noise. But it didn't take long for my two younger sisters to get on her nerves.

The fact that Sandy never had a sister of her own made her a devoted friend and confidant. I, on the other hand, needed an escape from the pressures and responsibilities of being the oldest and having to take care of a younger brother and two sisters. I was vanilla, and she was chocolate. We double-dated, ditched classes, read poetry and sang along to Diana Ross and the Supremes. We helped each other get through teenage heartaches, Algebra and a wide variety of family crisis. Sister-friends are a good thing to have at any age.

* * *

The "Wrestling with my Sister" title came from a Bible story of two sisters who wrestled for the affection of the same man. Their names were Leah and Rachel. Rachel hated Leah because in spite of the fact that Jacob was in love with Rachel, through a series of events, he ended up married to Leah.

In Genesis 29:31: When the Lord saw that Leah was hated, He opened her womb; but Rachel was barren. This scripture makes it very clear that God will not tolerate one sister hating another sister. A curse will come upon the one who is sending out a spirit of hatred. At the same time God will bless the woman who is hated and make her prosperous. He will give her a new job, a new man and perform miracles in her life. He will also do it right in front of the people who hate her the most.

Have you ever watched two women play the games of "I've got one up on you?" A single sister runs into a married sister in the grocery store. The married sister is busy trying to make her baby sit down in the basket, while her three year old is pulling cans off of the shelves. In the mind of the married woman, she is a sloppy mess with two wild children that she can't seem to quiet down. The single woman is wearing a business suit and has an expensive designer bag hanging from her shoulder. The married woman can see her new sports car parked next to her dented up van.

The single woman approaches her married friend feeling envious and frustrated as she looks at the two beauty-full children busy laughing and playing, while their mother is busy purchasing goodies for her big fine husband. They come together thinking how green the grass looks on the other side of their respective fences.

"It's so good to see you Tanya," the married sister flashes a broad smile.

"Shanika," you've got two kids and you haven't gained a pound. Girl you look good!" Tanya replies.

"Well, my husband and I try to spend some time walking together when he comes home in the evenings," Shanika explains.

"I wish I had time to walk in the evenings," Tanya explains. "But my new job has me traveling constantly. Those transcontinental flights to Asia and Europe are so hard on my body, I really have to get on some type of exercise program."

"Well my husband and I just moved into a house near a beautiful lake, so we just love walking near the water at sunset, it is so romantic. Do you have a boyfriend yet?" Shanika grins.

"Girl, you know how hard it is to find a man who

makes as much money as I do. I just had a date last weekend cruising on a man's yacht, but of course he's of a different racial persuasion."

In reality Tanya was feeling worn out and lonely from chasing her own tail. Although her career is moving up, she feels like she is going nowhere, because it's not what she really wants out of life. Her mother had convinced her if she got a good education, she could have her pick of eligible men. Of course, that was the farthest thing from the truth. What Tanya thinks she really wants is what Shanika has, a good husband and beauty-full kids to love. It is all she thinks about and nothing else really matters. To make matters worse, Tanya was still recovering from her boyfriend's sudden exit, after deciding that he wasn't ready for a serious commitment. "Why is life so complicated?" Tanya thought to herself. "Why can't I be like Shanika and have a man who really loves me and wants to take care of me?"

Shanika on the other hand is at her wits end. She dropped out of college to marry her sweetheart. Because she wasn't very skilled, she worked mediocre jobs to help make ends meet while her husband finished school. Once he graduated, and the children were born, she began to feel more like a maid and a baby-sitter than a happily married woman. To make matters worse, three months after they moved into their dream house, Shanika's husband lost his job. She felt even worse because she wasn't capable of getting a good job that could help get them out of the hole. "Why can't I be smart and talented like Tanya," she thinks to herself. "Why do I always look so disheveled? Tanya always looks so cool and sophisticated in her clothes."

Although the story of Tanya and Shanika are just a figment of my vivid imagination, I am certain that you can recognize or have been caught up in a real life drama of "my husband is doing better than your husband. My kids are smarter than your kids. I make more money than you do," and the beat goes on. Many of these situations can turn very serious and very deadly. I know of two blood sisters who have not spoken in ten years because of what began as a petty disagreement and exploded into a world war.

If Tanya and Shanika could have gotten past all the superficial stuff, they could have been a big help to each other. Shanika could have comforted Tanya about loosing her boyfriend. Maybe she could have even fixed her up with one of her husband's buddies.

Tanya, on the other hand, could have been there to calm Shanika's fears about loosing her house. Maybe she could have checked into an opening for Shanika's husband at her company, or helped Shanika find work.

After all, isn't that why God gave us sisters?

You are only hurting yourself if you put your energy into despising another woman because she has, or is:

•Younger
•Has the man you want
•Pretty hair
•Perfect skin
•Shapely body
•Fashion plate
•Good education
•Money
•Happily married
•Single and successful
•Powerful
•Rich husband
•Good children
•Talented
•Spiritual
•Leader

•Favor with people
•Beautiful home
•World traveler
•Famous
•Classy

If you delight in your sister and work through your differences, then God will bless you and your sister. There is no doubt in my mind that the key to the survival of the women who endured the pain of slavery, was the fact that they had no other choice but to stick together and pray for one another.

If you have been wounded by a sister-friend, or you know that you have been putting up a front with her, maybe it's time to put all the garbage in the can and get real with one another. Talk about the offenses. Talk about the facades. Alone is a very lonely place to be. We were made to be there for one another, to love one another, to help each other grow and be a model of love and relationships for the next generation.

* * *

Within the younger ranks of African-American women, the wrestling match continues. Too many women of color have been victimized by the paper bag test. If you're darker than a brown paper bag, you are too dark to be accepted into certain social circles. On the campuses of many Black Colleges, there is still strong evidence that certain sororities exercise a very discreet "color line." One group of sorority sisters appear very Creole, with extremely light complexions and straight or curly hair. Another group of sorority sisters look like a sea of coffee brown faces, sporting dreads, braids and twisted hairdos.

There's a belief system between them that is full of holes and half-truths. Yet, they continue to honor their myths.

The browner girls are supposed to be smarter and the lighter girls get first choice on the best guys. Light skin guys like the brown skinned girls. Dark skinned guys go after the lighter girls. The color of the Homecoming queen depends on the social climate of the campus at the given time. It may be a season where there is a very Afro-centric vibe. Therefore, the queen will be darker, with more African features. On the other hand it may be a time when everybody is doing the "Halle Berry" thing. Then the queen will have a "racially mixed" look about her.

What happens on Black campuses is only a reflection of what is going on in the general population of African-American sisterhood. It happens in offices, churches, social clubs and political groups. We are worse than the local gang-bangers accepting or rejecting one another because one group is wearing the color red and the other group is wearing the color blue. In reality, they are all brothers and sisters from the same race and tribe. The real enemy stands in the shadows rejoicing as they destroy one another.

"Sisters"

What you looking at girl?
You looking for that part of "you,"
that helps you relate to me?
You looking for that secret thing,
you wish that you could be?
In your mind, your hand is on your hip,
while you study me real good.
You scared I'm gonna steal your man,
like some kind of Robin Hood?
Will you please stop checkin out my hair, and take a look at
all my fears.
Can't you see that if we come together we can dry each

others tears.
I'm not so busy competing with you that I can't hear the
voice of God.
I know that I'm the blessing that you need,
and I'm holding it here inside.
I'm not a slave master trying to bind you up, or the hand that
beats you down.
We are simply two queens in a foreign land,
looking for our crowns.

Self imposed discrimination is nothing new among
African-American women. The wrestling matches between
sisters are frequently centered around the struggle over men,
or what is viewed as the "stuck up" behavior of light skinned
girls who think they're better than her coffee colored oppo-
nent. Or a "stuck up" coffee colored sister who rejects her
cream colored sister, just because she "don't like high yella
girls."

Sisters who wound one another's self-esteem by rejecting one another because of the color of their skin, or the
length of their hair, are unknowingly being loyal to the spirit of
slavery and the demon of division. Little girls who grow up as
the only light or dark one in the family, will harbor strong feelings of anger and resentment for being rejected by their own
family members.

Divide and conquer is still the cherry bomb that keeps
blowing us apart at a time when more than ever, we need to
come together.

In light of the challenges we now face, churches and
other organizations where women gather must evict the demon of division, and deal with real needs and real issues.

When we repent of our jealous and envious attitudes
toward one another, repent of our backbiting and competitive
spirits, affirm the beauty of our young sisters, respect and honor

the beauty of older women, then the true purpose and reward of sisterhood will begin to manifest.

* * *

As we discuss the issue of sisters hating sisters, I feel it is important to address the feelings of animosity between Black women and White women. Again, let me remind you that *any kind of hatred and negativity against anyone only keeps you from being blessed.* It is for this reason that I am dealing with the issue of racial prejudice.

It is important to note, that in the same way that African American women are judged by their physical appearance, White women are also valued by how they look. Blond hair, blue eyes, and petite bodies have always been the standard of beauty that White men have established for White women. Women of Russian and German descent often suffer rejection because of their big bones and awkward bodies. Women from Italy or Spain were ostracized for their olive skin and dark hair. I have known many White women who grew up feeling rejected because they did not have blond hair and or blue eyes like other members of the family. Or because there complexion was not white enough. Jewish women still face harsh discrimination in many parts of the world.

One of the main points of contention between Black women and White women is centered around relationships between Black men and White women. As if it's not difficult enough for a Black woman to find a Black man who is sane, in reasonable health and employed, White women now actively pursue and marry eligible Black males.

My daughter Theresa encountered an interracial couple on an airplane recently. She admitted to me that at first she was slightly irritated. But as she sat across from them, her feelings began to change. When Theresa needed a pillow, the man got out of his seat and found one for her. "I don't think he was trying to make some kind of statement, he was just a real nice guy."

During the trip, the three of them laughed and talked. By the time they had reached their destination, in spite of her personal feelings, Theresa was convinced that these two were probably made for each other.

Whether it is a real or imaged, the air of superiority that White women sometimes demonstrate, many times is an attempt to mask their own feelings of insecurity and rejection. It may also be a cultural gap that brings about a misunderstanding. We may expect a woman from another culture to respond to us a certain way. When they don't, we are offended.

Sometimes when I speak before a group of White women, they don't move, smile, or show any emotion. To me, they seem cold and distant. But once I finish speaking, they come to me weeping and chattering away about how much they enjoyed the message. Just as they sometimes don't understand our cultural traits, it is easy for us to misinterpret what is going on in their mind-set.

While it may appear that White women have many advantages that women of color are not privy to, a closer inspection will reveal that when it comes to trouble, there are different strokes for different folks.

I can still remember talking to a very nice White woman many years ago in Washington D.C. We were attending a Congressional breakfast together and we just started talking. Within minutes she shared with me that her husband was a trucking tycoon. She lived on an estate somewhere in North or South Carolina. Suddenly the tears began to roll down her face as she shared how her daughter's feelings of isolation and rejection had led her to commit suicide the year before. I took her hand as we sat down together in a deserted hallway. We talked for a long time and prayed together. Like my mother used to say, "everything that glitters ain't gold."

The main problems that Black women have with White women are simple: Unfair employment opportunities and scooping up eligible Black men. In reality, women from all kinds of background are looking for a good man, and if he happens to be Black, well, that's life!

Just as American automobile manufacturers must now compete with foreign auto makers, Black women must do all they can to become "the beauty-full flower with all the power." When Diana Ross married a White business tycoon who reportedly has assets in the billions, all I could say is "more power to the flower!"

I implore Black women to release any feelings of hatred toward women of any other racial group. All women struggle with the issues of liberation and acceptance. Women are denied education in parts of India and the Middle East. In Ethiopia, women are starving to death. In Russia and Bosnia, women face political oppression. Right here in America, women struggle to exist on government subsidies or work on a job that barely meets her expenses. These women are Black, Native American, White, Hispanic and Asian.

African-American women can learn many important lessons by observing women from other racial groups. A good example can be seen in how Asian women work together. They will open a small manicure and pedicure shop in a Black neighborhood. Starting with one or two operators, in a short period of time they manage to build a booming business.

These women are success-full because they work harder than anybody else and they try to get along with one another. They are polite and accommodating to customers. They will stay open from the first thing in the morning to the late hours of the night to finish their work. They will keep working just as long as we are willing to pay for their services. Very rarely do you find Asian children in a day care center. The older women and young girls watch the children care for the house and prepare the food while the adult women work outside of the home.

White women also have something to offer. They have excellent communication skills when it comes to dealing with men. They are also masters of self-control. They know how to stay focused on their goal without getting side tracked by their emotions. I come from a very emotional family where the women are quick to "give you a piece of their mind." In the business world, that is not always a good idea. I have learned from observing Caucasian women the fine art of staying calm and speaking in a soft tone of voice even when the circumstances make you want to scream at the top of your lungs.

Hispanic women love family unity. Whether they are in the grocery store or riding down the street, it is not unusual to see the husband, wife, grandmother, grandfather and all the children piled into one car. They don't mind sharing their home with cousins, aunts, uncles and friends. Everyone works together sharing their money and possessions. It is this way of life that has allowed Hispanics to become the fastest growing minority in America.

African-American women bring another kind of beauty to the table, especially in the area of mothering and teaching children. We are the masters of perseverance, patience, and endurance. While women from other racial persuasions crumble under the pressures of life, African-American women smile and keep going. Even during times of slavery and segregation, we found the strength to comfort the White women who should have been comforting us. Only recently have we allowed nervous breakdowns to "break us down." We had our breakdowns, but never took a break. We scrapped, saved and sold chicken dinners on Sunday after church to build Black colleges and churches so our children could have a better life.

Years ago we accomplished more even though we

had less. Today we have better jobs, but we have not yet built new colleges or done more than our grandmothers to help our people. I am convinced that we are not hindered by the issue of money, but of unity.

All women are beauty-full and full-of-beauty in their own way. But inner-beauty can only been seen through the eyes of love.

* * *

I believe that when sisters unite together, our children will no longer be murdered in the streets.

I believe that when sisters work together, we will no longer be enslaved by poverty.

I believe that when sisters pray together, our men will be set free from prisons and marriages will be saved.

I believe that when sisters fast together, the power of drug addiction will be broken in our communities.

I believe that when sisters weep together, we will see each other's needs and be healed from our hurts.

I believe that when sisters stand together, God will stand with us against racial and political injustices.

I believe that when sisters repent together, we will return to moral excellence, decency and purity.

I believe that when sisters walk together, our children will follow in our footsteps and live successful, prosperous and Godly lives.

* * *

Raising Little Women

For me, there is no greater task then preparing little girls to become godly, confident and beauty-full women. I wholeheartedly agree with the philosophy that it indeed takes a whole village to raise one child. We all have a part in raising beauty-full children, and it is never too early to start.

Whenever I see a young child, no matter how they are dressed or how they look, I treat them like they are very special, because they are. I always look them in their little face and tell them that they are beauty-full. I tell them they have nice hair and pretty skin. I tell them I like their eyes, their nose and their lips. I like to tell them how smart they are and how good they are.

Even when they are doing something wrong, I am always careful of how I bring correction. For example, I will say; "I can't believe a good boy like you is acting this way," or, "You are so smart, I know you can do better work if you want too." Always base your corrections on their behavior and not their person.

It is also important that parents don't allow family conflicts to ruin a child's self image. Never say in a negative way, "You act just like your father, or you remind me of your mother, and you know how awful she is or he is."

Never abuse a child physically or with words. Don't call them stupid, black or ugly. Don't make fun of them, especially when they are attempting to do something right.

You don't have to be a mother to get involved in a child's development. Work with your nieces, nephews, cousins, or children in your church or neighborhood.

It is important that you help them identify their gifts and talents. Get them involved in sports, music, science workshops and public speaking. Put them in the children's choir at church or the junior usher board. All of these activities not only help them to discover their talents, but also build their self-confidence and self esteem. If a child is not being properly taken care of, you may be able to help.

If the opportunity presents itself, help a little girl understand the importance of good grooming. If possible, make sure she keeps her hair neatly braided or curled, especially before going to school or church.

Tell her about the importance of bathing, deodorant, and wearing clean and neat clothing. If possible, buy your little girl friend a cosmetic kit with personal items inside, like deodorant, toothpaste, a comb and brush. If the opportunity presents itself, give her information about her menstrual cycle. Many neglected little girls are totally unprepared for the physical and emotional trauma of starting their period. Let her know that she must try to look, act and feel like a beauty-full princess at all times.

Nine years ago the Lord blessed me with a beauty-full granddaughter. We named her Ashley Jade Ballard. I also have two wonderful, marvelous grandsons. Adam McFaddin Ballard is the oldest. He wants to make films. He is a very special young man. Anthony Andrew is the youngest. He seems to have a gift for music, but time will tell.

I want to focus on Ashley because we are talking about raising little women. Just before her 9th birthday, I began making plans to celebrate the nine years of joy that she has brought to our family. Ashley is very special and full-of-beauty. I wanted her to know without a doubt that she is loved and valued.

She arrived at my house on the afternoon of her birthday to find a stack of presents covering the coffee table. Her eyes were wide with excitement. She opened the biggest box first. Inside was a beautiful white party dress with pearls, "T" straps and a matching white shawl. Inside of another box was a pearl necklace, matching pearl earrings and two gold rings.

She opened another box and another. There was a beautiful corsage made with real pink roses and baby's breath. There was a new white purse to match her dress. Inside the purse she found money and three tickets to see "Beauty And The Beast" at the Shubert Theater. Her mother and I fixed her hair, put on her new dress, picked up her little friend and headed for the theater. Afterwards, the whole family met her for dinner and dessert at her favorite restaurant. She fell asleep that night with a permanent smile on her face.

Did we overdo it? Maybe we did, but as my mother use to say, "every child is entitled to a childhood." We want Ashley Jade to know how much she means to our family. We want her to grow up believing that she is valuable and special. That is why we took the time to build her self-esteem by celebrating her birthday in a very special way.

Little girls should be made to feel beauty-full. If at all possible, they should be taken out by their fathers and treated like the lady that she hopes to become some day.

The issue of hair and skin color among African American girls can be critical to their self-esteem. If it hurts when I get my hair combed, then surely there must be something "bad" about my hair. If she never see's a dark complexioned girl play the part of a princess or finds a Black girl on the cover of a magazine, then it must not be good to have a dark complexion.

This is the conclusion that many little girls come to at a very early age.

My granddaughter Ashley has very thick, coarse, coffee brown hair. When she was younger, she hated to get her hair combed because it was so painful. Her mother kept it in braids so it wouldn't need to be combed everyday. We had to work hard to convince Ashley that she was blessed to have a head full of thick, coarse hair. We never used words like "nappy" or "bad hair." My motto is, if you have any hair at all... it's good hair!

Raising my daughter Roslyn, Ashley's mother, presented a completely different set of challenges. Roz is my adopted daughter. I married her father when she was seven years old. Her father had several unsuccessful relationships, including a divorce from Roslyn's mother. This little girl had a deep fear of being rejected. She didn't think that she was very lovable. Her hair was broken and badly damaged. She also had a rotten attitude, which was her way of protecting a heart that had been wounded so many times.

"This is my house!" she announced the first time her father left us alone together. "So don't you try to tell me what to do!"

Adam, my new husband was scheduled to pick us up in one hour. My instructions were to get Roz and myself dressed so he could take us out to dinner.

"I'm not taking a bath and I'm not getting dressed," she shouted with her arms folded across her chest.

Without one word, I whacked her on her bottom, and escorted her into the bathroom. I didn't hit her hard enough to inflict pain, but to let her know who was the boss. After I gave her a bath, I hugged her and fixed her hair in a pretty style.

"Can I call you mommy?" Roz asked me before we left the house. We have been in love with each other ever since.

In the years that followed, I took the time to grow

her hair and her self-esteem. Both were badly damaged. I enrolled her in ballet lessons and took her to class every Saturday. Once, while she was taking a lesson, I went to get a cup of coffee. When I came back, she was hysterical and out of breath. She thought that I had left her and was never coming back. From that day forward, I was careful to keep my word, never break a promise, and reassure her every day that I would never leave her. Even if I was going through a difficult period with her father, I never allowed it to affect my relationship with Roz. I made her my confidante and best friend.

Recently, I was talking to a friend named John who had gone through a painful divorce. He was sharing with me that a close friend was going through a similar experience.

"He wanted me to give him some advice," John explained. "But what could I say to him when my marriage had also failed?"

"I think you have a lot to say," I argued. "You can tell your friend that although your heart was broken, with time, God healed your emotions."

"You can tell him that through all the confusion, you focused on the welfare of your children. You were there for them. You understood their pain and helped them work through it."

"You can tell him how you rebuilt your life and the lives of your children. You gave them a home and the emotional stability that they needed," I added.

John was quiet for a long time before he spoke. "I guess things could have been a lot worse. Thank God the kids are doing good and their mother and I are becoming friends again."

When parents divorce, kids don't necessarily have to live in a "broken home." A "broken home" is a place where nothing is working. All too often, married couples living together with children are living in a "broken home."

Today, many children come from divorced homes, foster homes, or grow up with alcoholic or drug addicted parents. Any and all of these circumstances can cause a child to grow up full of confusion, shame and low self-esteem.

Children who have become victims of divorce often feel responsible for the break up of the family. To make matters worse, the children feel like they are an unwanted responsibility.

Fatherless little girls frequently look for men who can be a father figure. Girls who grow-up with abusive fathers will be drawn to abusive men. Girls who have been sexually abused become promiscuous, or because of their fear of men, turn to lesbian relationships. One evening at church, I talked with a girl who was dressed in men's clothing. After the service, we talked about her deep hurts.

"I was molested by my mother's boyfriend," she said. "I don't want to be a woman because, men think they can take advantage of me again."

It is important that everyone in the "village" participate in keeping children safe, and making broken children whole again. This can be accomplished in the following ways:

1. Listen patiently while the child talks their head off. This makes them believe that what they think and feel is important. If you won't listen to them, a predator will.

2. Even if you are not a parent, visit their school. Talk to their teacher. This means that someone is concerned about them.

3. Be a special guest when they have an activity, like a school play or a sporting event.

4. Remember them at Christmas and on their birthday. Don't worry about the expense. A card with a dollar inside sends a clear message of love and affection.

5. Let a child hang out with you, even if you're not really doing anything. Take your little 'homey' to the park, church, the mall, or the library.

6. You don't have to be the solution to every problem. Just being there is enough.

7. Tell them about God. Help to build their faith and belief in what their eyes cannot see. This will give them inner strength.

Any and all of these simple acts of kindness and caring can help a little girl grow into a woman who is full of beauty and beauty-full.

* * *

In Full Bloom

All normal, healthy, young women have a built-in "rite of passage." Once a female starts her menstrual cycle, she becomes an official card carrying member of the international society of womanhood. The *teen years* are, without a doubt, one of the most difficult periods in a woman's life. Her body goes through a rapid and sometimes embarrassing transition. Her skin may break out or become too oily or dry. Her body seems to be bloated, and her mood can change at the drop of a hat. This period is sometimes called "the ugly duckling phase."

A teenage girl is never sure who will be in the mirror when she wakes up. She goes to sleep with a flat chest and wakes up with breast and red spots in her underwear. It's enough to frighten the bravest of the bunch. For this reason, we must be more supportive than ever before. We need every mother, grandmother, aunt, big sister and all other available women to help stop the wave of young girls who are in such need of acceptance that they are willing to expose themselves to a dreaded disease, or have an abortion or baby that they are not prepared to raise.

Love, support and validation will keep a young woman in bloom from blowing the mission. The family and the village must come up with a plan to save our young women from being thrown to the wolves. Teenagers will not only set goals for themselves, but they will reach them, if someone is there to remind them how the game really goes.

In high school, the most important thing next to trying to graduate is the discovery of boys. Every young girl wants to be loved and accepted. Every young boy secretly wants the same thing. The scary part is how teenagers define love and acceptance.

The national anthem of every young boy who's hoping to score, or find acceptance, is: "If you love me you will..." He is also following his natural male instinct to hunt down and conquer. Not only is he out to conquer her body, but he wants her mind as well. His esteem is built on a shaky house of cards. When he gets his "mack" down and girls start telling him that he's the greatest thing on earth, for that moment, he sees himself safely perched on the top of the mountain.

More and more, I run into mothers, many of them single, who are granting their sons their every wish.

"Ah, come on mom!" the young man whines. And because he is so sweet and so cute, mommy grants her little boy all that he desires. Tennis shoes that cost hundreds of dollars, gold jewelry and expensive jeans. Retailers report that teens literally spend billions of dollars annually on designer labeled clothing and accessories.

The problem with mom being so generous, instead of making her son Jabari earn his keep, this young man is putting the same beg on his young girlfriend. That's why he goes after her mind, as well as her body.

A young girl who is fearful of facing rejection will not only give Jabari money for those Air Jordans or Nikes, but will participate in sex, not for the sake of sex, but for acceptance. Without intervention, a teenage girl can sacrifice her whole future for a boy who will use her like she's a plastic cup.

His only goal is to take a drink to satisfy his thirst, then throw her in the trash. The same boy is on to the next conquest, while she is stuck with a baby, an abortion, a broken heart, a disease or all of the above. Even if he sticks around, he is probably not mature enough, nor does he have the resources to help her reach her full potential as a woman.

Not only is she desperate to be accepted by the boy of her dreams, but she wants to fit in with her girlfriends. Therefore, she does what she thinks everybody else is doing so she won't feel like she's on the outside looking in.

The only way to keep her from being pimped out of the money she makes on her part-time job, or the money her parents are giving her, is for someone who is mature and stable to love her and appreciate her more than her peers, who are probably just as lost and love starved. This young girl deserves a better role model than Mary J. Blidge. She's a singer who appears on MTV wearing a blonde wig, dark sunglasses and a span-dex skirt. While that sexy, "freak thing" image is definitely in, the pied-pipers of gangsta-rap and x-rated soul music are leading young girls to a very tragic end. Yes, in our day, the O.G.s (old gangsters - *smile*) had their fun too, but it didn't end in drug addiction, drive-by shootings, multiple sex partners and rampant teen pregnancies.

If you're still in your teens, don't be deceived into thinking that you can handle things, and you don't need adults telling you what to do with your life. The proof of the need for guidance can be seen in all the funerals of young people that I have attended. In this year alone I have only been to one funeral where the person was over twenty-five.

Peer pressure is very real. A young woman in need of love and acceptance will constantly search for a way to fill the void in her life. A caring family, big sister or a strong youth group will keep her from having to deal with the pain of rejection and keep her moving in a safe direction.

The survival of teenage girls is resting on the willingness of grown women to see the need and fill it. If you are the parent of a teenage girl, don't expect her to be what you are not. If you want her to hold on to her virginity, then don't live a promiscuous life-style. If you want her to stay away from drugs, don't bring alcohol into your house. She is looking for a woman that she can model. Someone to show her the right way. As her mother, God intended for you to be that model. Other women around you should be there to support your efforts.

Don't set your daughter up to be raped or molested. If you are not married, be careful of your men friends that want to spend time with her. Talk to her about intimate things. Teach her how to conduct herself with boys and with men. Never allow her to take expensive gifts from boys. Don't let her sit on a man's lap. When she is wearing a dress, make sure she keeps her legs down. If something is going on that makes her uncomfortable, she should feel free to talk to you openly. Don't let her "hang out" with people that you don't know well. Check on her stories, even if she starts ranting and raving about her privacy and trusting her. Pick her up from the mall, practice, and parties even though she complains that she doesn't want to be treated like a baby.

When my daughters were in their teens, they hung out with me, more than their friends. I wanted not only to be a parent, but a friend to my girls. When Theresa went to her prom, we all went to the prom. I chaperoned. Her sister Roz and her date doubled with Theresa and her date. We were all so close, she didn't mind having us along. I don't know what her date was planning, but it sure didn't include sex.

As a parent, grandparent, aunt, or big sister, it is important to help your teen girl(s) build her confidence and feel good about herself. This is a very difficult time in a girls life. *We must do everything in our power to develop the beauty-full woman that is hiding on the inside.*

If she's not the prom queen type, then help her win the essay contest. If she doesn't like talking in front of people, find out if she's interested in sports. I have a niece named Jenni, who I love dearly. She is a big girl for her age. For a long time, she was taller and stronger than most of the boys in her class. Her size could have made her feel awkward and out of place, but my sister Lil did the wise thing and got Jenni involved in sports. She immediately found her niche. Whenever she had a soccer game, the whole family showed up to cheer for her. We call her our future Olympic champion.

Help a young girl find her niche. As she begins to pour herself into the thing that she loves doing, she will feel a lot better about herself and will have a lot less time to get into trouble.

Young girls must see models of adult women who are not only talking the talk, but walking the walk. Because I have daughters, nothing delights me more than a young girl who tells me that she wants to be like me when she grows up. When teens send me pictures or write me letters, I call them on the phone, or take them to the mall to hang out, when time permits. I have a special affection for teen girls living in foster care. Some of the most beauty-full and talented girls on earth have no families of their own to love them.

I encourage every adult woman who has a home to share and love to give, to take a foster child under your roof. You will be blessed beyond measure. If that isn't possible, think about getting involved with a youth group, or starting a program, or having activities centered around young people. Give cooking lessons, or lessons on etiquette. Make a quilt together, or start a writer's workshop. Whatever your gift is, share it with young people. One woman in her forties blew me away. She not only started a community choir on her own, but the teens also performed dance and pantomime. In my spare time I do wall hangings with kids. We pick themes and everybody gets to participate.

Three things that I believe teenage girls need in order to become success-full and productive women.

1. LOVE - A strong family support system, including a caregiver or mentor who is involved in their development.

2. GOD - A church and youth fellowship that challenges them to be spiritually and morally excellent.

3. EDUCATION - Academic training as well as recognizing and developing their special gifts and talents.

* * *

Pouring In
The Power

*Who can find a virtuous woman? For she is
more valuable than rubies. Proverbs 31:10*

The word "virtuous" comes from the Latin word
"virtus," which means strength, power and courage. The word
"virtuous" is used to describe a woman who has become power-
full by living a life of moral and spiritual excellence.

Once you embrace the life-style of the virtuous
woman, you become the recipient of God's power. In order to
maintain the power that is poured into you, it will be necessary
to reject all that is evil and ungodly. Sin is like "cryptonite"
that spiritually cripples and drains the virtuous woman.

The power that is poured into you is practical and
tangible. It can be applied to your daily life as you face the
smallest and greatest obstacles. You have the power within
you to stand against destructive forces designed to destroy your
life and the lives of the people around you. Any weakness of
the flesh or spirit can cause your container of power to develop
leaks. Your spiritual goal should be to seal up every leaky area
that might leave you power-less instead of power-full. The
closer you get to God, the stronger you will become in the areas of self-discipline and self-control.

By fasting and purifying your mind and body of items and ideas that are polluted, your spiritual antenna gets higher and higher. You develop x-ray vision and hearing, enabling you to see and read thoughts and intentions of people and situations surrounding you. Living in the supernatural realm becomes very natural as you grow closer to God. You will gain inner strength and become more power-full as you continue to exercise your spiritual muscles in prayer and faith. You will have the courage to withstand upsets, and crisis of every kind, without losing your cool or becoming unstable. You will be an invincible fortress against the attacks aimed at your family, friends and your personal goals. As you rebuke the enemy in prayer, the plots and obstacles that come against you and your family eventually disintegrate into thin air. People around you who are trapped in addiction, confusion, poverty and sickness, will find the power to break free.

Please note as you face the attacks of the enemy, that two of the greatest attributes of power are *patience* and *endurance*. When you become a power-full woman, you stand your ground and keep standing. You are a "how-ever-long-it-takes," kind of woman. In this fax sending, fast food, microwave, jet setting age, most people have lost the fine art of patience. With all of the progress surrounding us, when we pray, we want the answer to come instantly, immediately and right now! It takes faith and power to patiently wait for God's perfect plan and God's perfect timing. Many of you are the recipients of the supernatural power of your mother's and grandmother's prayers. Only God knows how patiently they waited for you to see the light.

Spiritual battles are fought in many different arenas. A woman with a solid education and work history encounters the corporate "glass ceiling." A devoted wife discovers her husband is having an affair. A child gets into trouble. When promises are broken, negotiations fail, and you run out of natu-

ral answers and natural resources, you will become more focused than ever on the God of all power.

Many times it appears that the virtuous woman doesn't
have the strength to deal with a difficult situation. But a woman
who walks with the living God has more power than meets the
eye. Under her silk blouse, you will find "Superwoman" written across her chest. She may not be able to move a piano
across the room, but in the spirit realm, she can move mountains.

Just as E=mc2, the formula developed by Albert
Einstein for atomic energy, holiness must be factored into the
power equation. Holiness + Faith = Power. It is unfortunate
that most women do not understand the real value of living a
"holy" life. In recent times, "holiness" has gotten a bad rap, so
to speak. You've heard the term, "Miss holier than thou!" Or
"Holy roller." The truth of the matter is that holiness simply
means "to be made whole," or to remove all the things that
would break, bruise, fracture, splinter or soil your mind, your
emotions, your body, and your spirit.

Once you become "whole" or holy, God can pour tremendous amounts of power into your clean, sanctified, "leak
proof" vessel. In order to stand toe to toe and overcome adver-
sities, you must be power-packed. To be holy doesn't mean
that you don't make mistakes, or that you are 100% bona-fide,
Patty Perfect. It simply means that you are "wholly" and completely committed to God's transforming Word which is designed
to help you become a power-full woman capable of rising above
every obstacle.

Women who reject the spiritual laws and boundaries
of holiness may succeed for a while, but will always end up
frustrated and power-less. I have lost count of the women who
have come to me asking for my help. They want my counsel
and they want my prayers. They want to escape from their
problems, but when I explain to them the changes that God

requires them to make, many of these women chose to suffer rather than to change their life-style.

At first I use to grieve over the women who became victims of their own rebellion. It was like trying to keep a blind man from walking off a cliff. It took many years of feeling frustrated before I realized that I could only help the people who really want to be helped. Then and only then can power be released and utilized effectively.

Contrary to popular opinion, the woman who practices the "beauty of holiness" in her life-style wears makeup, jewelry, fashionable hairstyles and clothing. But while she appears to be sophisticated and in step with the rest of the world, she is definitely marching to the beat of a different drummer.

She is knowledgeable about legislation and social trends that are destructive to our families and communities. She refuses to compromise her beliefs and is aggressive in promoting the principles and practices spelled out in the Word of God.

I encourage you to become a woman of prayer. A woman of prayer is a woman of power. Pray about everything. Make a list of people and situations that you are praying over. If you are a morning person, find a quiet place to have "quiet time" with the Lord. Many women use the bathroom or the kitchen. I personally like to pray outside while I walk. That way I am not interrupted by people or ringing telephones.

Ephesians 3:20 (Living) reads: Now glory be to God who by His might power at work within us is able to do far more than we would ever dare to ask or even dream of - infinitely beyond our highest prayers, desires, thoughts, or hopes. Don't be afraid of being the object of ridicule and criticism for your "strange" practices and behavior. A woman who is holy and virtuous can take the heat and live to enjoy the fruits of her righteous living.

No matter how power-less you may feel, there is an untapped power source inside of each of us. "His mighty power is at work within us." Sometimes it takes just the right challenge or circumstance that has your back against the wall for you to come out swinging. Many women who thought of themselves as weak were almost swallowed up, but managed to find the power switch and hit the "on" button. They prevailed!

For those women who knowingly walk in power, I believe there are levels of power "at work within us" that have yet to be tapped. As you grow and face new challenges in life, you will either tuck your tale in retreat, or find the "on" switch that will take you to a higher level of power. African American history is rich with stories of Black women who found the "on" switch and became the vessels of God's power. These women defied every standard of what our society considers attractive and powerful. They were underprivileged and disadvantaged, yet they prevailed.

Sojourner Truth was born into slavery in 1797. Her slave name was Isabella Baumree, better known as "Belle." For many years she quietly performed her duties of washing, ironing and caring for her master's children. By age fourteen, she married and gave birth to five children. It is a well known fact that one of her children was fathered by her master. She was an ordinary woman, but something extraordinary was at work on the inside.

During a prayer meeting in 1843, she accepted Jesus Christ as Lord of her life and was called to preach the gospel. Isabella Baumfree later wrote that while she was ironing a pile of clothes, she asked the Lord what she should do? "The Lord told me that He wanted me to be a sojourner, spreading truth throughout the land. After I met the Lord, I knew I wasn't just another slave woman. I was a different person, so I took a different name... Sojourner Truth."

In the years that followed, she became a fiery abolitionist, preaching, encouraging and sometimes raising more money than the renowned anti-slavery activist, Frederick Douglass. Once when he became discouraged, Sojourner told him, "don't lose heart... God is not dead!"

Audiences of all races and social backgrounds were spellbound as she preached the gospel and lectured against the evils of slavery. Sojourner was so tall and rugged looking that she was accused of masquerading as a woman. To put an end to the gossip, she angrily stripped to the waist in public to show her breast.

When one of her son's was illegally sold, she sued the slave owner and forced him to return her son. While living in Washington, D.C., she nursed the sick, raised money and found employment for slaves who had escaped from the South. She eventually was called to the White House where she received the support of President Abraham Lincoln. In 1870, she developed a plan under which the federal government was to set aside land in the West for Blacks to develop. She died without ever seeing the plan implemented, but clearly used the power she was given to change the face of American history.

Harriet Ross Tubman, better known as "Black Moses," helped hundreds of slaves escape to freedom. This Black woman was radical and power-full. She was born in Bucktown, Maryland during the 1820's. At age 13, she received a serious blow on the head for fighting with a overseer who was beating one of the slaves. For the rest of her life she experienced blackouts, but her condition never hindered her mission. The story is told that she could clearly hear the voice of God telling her exactly what to do to guide her people to freedom. She claimed that the Lord revealed to her, who could be trusted and when she was in danger. If any of the slaves that she was taking to freedom became fearful and tried to go back to the plantation, she threatened to kill them to protect the others. Her father gave her a knowledge of the woods which later

helped her make 19 successful missions, leading over 300 slaves
to free northern states and into Canada.

Bounty hunters searching for runaway slaves stretched
from the deep South all the way into Canada, but the Lord guided
this fearless woman around every one of them. She never lost
one man, woman or child that traveled with her. The song "Wade
In The Water," was written about Harriet Tubman and the Un-
derground Railroad.

It was the Civil War that clearly demonstrated the
power of this woman warrior. She served as a nurse, scout and
spy for the Union Army. But in 1863 Tubman herself became
the military mind that led a union raid. More than 700 slaves
were set free under her leadership. For her acts of defiance, a
$40,000 reward was on her head, but this power-full woman
was never captured.

Mary McLeod Bethune was truly one of the great
women of African American history. Her ebony skin, silver
hair and gentle smile became the symbols of her power and
dedication. She was born in 1875 in the town of Mayesville,
South Carolina. She devoted her life to creating educational
opportunities for young Black Americans. Mary Bethune clearly
loved God and was full of His divine power. She attended a
seminary and graduated from the Moody Bible Institute with
the hope of becoming a missionary to Africa. Her dreams of
teaching African children how to read and write were shattered
when white church leaders refused to sponsor her as a missionary. However, what was meant for evil, eventually became a
blessing in disguise. Mary McLeod Bethune, the daughter of
former slaves found her mission right in her own backyard.
After recovering from her disappointment, it became clear that
her call in life was to provide education and guidance to Black
children.

In 1904, she opened a school for girls in Daytona

Beach, Florida. With the help of her husband Albertus Bethune, she pulled broken chairs and tables from trash piles and repaired them. She sold dinners and went from door to door asking for donations to keep the school open. She started with five students and grew to three hundred. The school was so successful that in 1923, it merged with a boy's school and became Bethune-Cookman College.

Mary McLeod Bethune's efforts proved without a doubt that academic preparation plus spiritual dedication could produce a generation of successful and power-full Black Americans. She went on to serve as advisor to four presidents and held several government posts in her lifetime. She served as Roosevelt's Special Advisor on Minority Affairs and later became the Director of the National Youth Administration. In 1935, she received the Spingard Medal and founded the National Council of Negro Women. The ripples of her power and influence can be felt until this very day.

* * *

Many African Americans know the names of the women who laid the foundation for the privileges that we now enjoy. But I fear that we have lost sight of why our spiritual grandmothers were able to accomplish superhuman feats.

Sojourner Truth liberated the souls of Blacks and Whites by preaching truth. Harriet Tubman liberated the lives of Black people by leading them to freedom. Mary McLeod Bethune liberated the minds of Black people by giving them education. None of these women were strangers to the principles of "holiness." Their lives bore witness to the fact that their strength and courage came from divine power being poured into their leakproof vessels.

We can only begin to imagine the physical, mental and emotional pain that our foremothers must have endured.

There was power, but there was also suffering. We sometimes operate under the illusion that because God is with us and empowered us, we are exempt from suffering. It is clear to me that suffering can be the very instrument that is used to develop our power.

We are instructed to endure hardness as good soldiers. Endurance means to suffer without surrendering. All too often we view suffering as a negative experience. But every adversity that we are allowed to experience only helps to build the muscles of determination. In the end, we are transformed into women of power.

Fear becomes Faith.

Weaknesses become weapons.

Discouragement becomes determination.

Failures become fortitude.

Pain becomes power.

Every woman who sees herself as ordinary has the potential to be extraordinary. You can be an extraordinary wife, parent, student, coach, community activist, teacher, or foster parent. These are only a few of the avenues that will allow you to become an extraordinary woman of power. Mother Hale, founded the Hale House because she was willing to take care of babies with AIDS. The world thought her love was extraordinary. When Dr. Mae Jeminson was a young girl she prayed and asked the Lord to let her fly. She became the first African American female astronaut. Marian Wright Edelman, head of the Children's Defense Fund wrote: "Lord, help me not to be a getter but a giver."

When my youngest daughter was in high school there was a sign hanging on her bedroom wall that said: "Few people rise above mediocrity because they are not willing to make the sacrifice that greatness calls for."

I had the privilege of knowing a power-full woman who successfully rose above mediocrity. She was millionaire, philanthropist, Eula McClainey. She was born in Mississippi and only had a sixth grade education. She came to Los Angeles, California with two small children and found work taking care of the disabled. In the years that followed, she opened a board and care home for senior citizens. The business grew and soon she owned several homes and invested in real estate. Eula McClainey went on to become one of the wealthiest African American women in the nation. A few years before she died, she was asked to speak at a conference. I will never forget her words as she shared her secrets of success.

"An education is not a magic wand," she began. "But it will help you along the way. I hire educated people all the time," she smiled. "The real secret of success is to let God open doors for you. Your job is to work as hard as you can once the doors have been opened." She ended her speech with a prayer that surprised most of the people in the room. She raised her arms and said: "Lord, may the spirit of *hard work* fall on all of these dear people. In Jesus name I pray, Amen!"

Governments flex their power muscles and the price of gold and silver fluctuates on the stock exchange. Powerful personalities come on the scene and captivate the world. But there are still spiritual laws that govern power that will never change.

- All human power has human limitations.
- Divine power is unlimited power.
- Divine power begins where human power ends.
- Access to divine power comes through faith in God.
- The demonstration of divine power glorifies God.

* * *

Celebration of a New Creation

A close friend wrote in the lyrics of a song: *"Until the pain of staying the same is greater than the pain of change, you won't... change!"* The process of transformation is a decision that must be made in your heart of hearts. It is a long and sometimes difficult process that does not happen overnight. At first the mind will resist the concept of becoming a new creation. The voice of negativity will try to tell you that nothing has changed. Those who are fearful of being left without a partner, in their "pity party," will find ways to discourage you and make you believe that your new goals have no real merit. It may hurt, but when it does, just remember the lyrics of the song: "Until the pain of staying the same is greater than the pain of change, you won't... change."

The enemy will try to convince you that the truths that God has revealed to you are nothing more than "pie in the sky," or something you can deal with later on in your life. But as you set your heart to practice the principles that are based on spiritual truths, the butterfly that is growing inside of you will slowly break through the cocoon. The Apostle Paul describes the struggle perfectly in Philippians 3:13: *(Paraphrased) But one thing I do: I forget about what is behind me and "press" forward to reach the goals that lie ahead.*

Don't "Stress" - "Press!" When we "stress" to make something happen, we are using negative energy. We are doing something that we don't really want to do and we don't really enjoy doing. This leads to weariness and frustration. When we "press" toward our goal, we are using positive energy. Even though what we are doing is difficult and full of challenges, we enjoy the work because it's what we really love to do.

God wants our transformation to be joyful in spite of the challenges that we must face. Once you discover the beauty-full woman living inside, then you can celebrate her existence by decorating the outside. Be sure to do a weekly manicure and pedicure. Dress yourself in the finest silks and satins. Size doesn't matter. Adorn yourself with gold, silver and jewels. Anoint yourself with the best perfumes and ointments reflecting the sweetness of your transformed soul.

When you go to bed at night, go to bed in lovely garments. When you rise in the morning, rise up with thanksgiving to the God who created you. Thank Him for making you so beauty-full and for giving you health and strength. Thank Him for the blessings that are finding their way to you and will soon overtake you. Ask Him to use you as a vessel to help others. Thank God for the beauty-full man in your life, whether he is presently in your life, in the process of being transformed, or on his way to you. Pray for your sisters, your brothers and your children. Ask the Lord to bless them and meet all of their needs. Then cleanse, groom and cover yourself with beauty-full things.

Braid, twist, curl, or blow dry your hair. Hair is a woman's crowning glory and should be treated with care and respect. Healthy hair should have a natural shine. The strands should be reasonably strong and free of breakage. The scalp should be smooth and free from flakes, scabs or rashes. The following tips will help you keep your hair beauty-full:

•Drink 6 to 8 glasses of spring or distilled water daily.
•Cleanse your scalp and rinse thoroughly on a regular basis.
•Whether your hair is worn natural, pressed or permed, don't us heavy grease and oils. They clog the pores of your scalp.
•Don't use sponge rollers, they cause breakage. Sleeping on a satin pillowcase helps prevent hair breakage.
•Eat iron rich high fiber food.
•Be sure to supplement your diet with vitamins, minerals and herbs.
•Create a stress free environment. Too much stress will cause hair loss.
•Wear a hairstyle that boldly expresses the real you.

Let your vital organs know that you love and appreciate them too. Eat foods that are good for you. Trash the junk foods and replace them by keeping fruit, natural juices and energy bars in your frige, desk and purse. Eat early in the day to avoid night time hunger pains. Eating late at night is a big no-no! Because of mineral erosion in the soil, even when we eat a healthy diet, many of the foods have been depleted of the nutrients that our bodies need. Therefore, I highly recommend that you explore the benefits of adding vitamins, minerals, and herbs to your daily diet. They are designed to help the body in the following ways:

•Cleanses the bowels and blood of toxins.
•Provides nutrition for the entire body.
•Normalizes bodily functions and the menstrual cycle.
•Raises energy level of the body.
•Stimulates the body's immune system.
•Helps the body to shed excess weight.
•Creates mental alertness.

I also recommend that you purchase the following books: *Vitamins and Minerals from A to Z* by Jewel Pookrum, M.D., Ph.D., *African Holistic Health* by Llaila O. Afrika, and *Herbally Yours*, by Penny C. Royal. There are also many other good books on the market. Be sure to exercise on a regular basis. Take the stairs instead of the elevator. Park your car in a place that will allow you to walk a good distance. Learn how to rest and relax, even if it means sitting in a nearby park. Take a dance or exercise class. Walk, or do floor exercises if you are feeling stressed.

Don't disrespect your lungs and heart with cigarettes. Drugs send a clear message to the brain and every part of your inner-self that you have no regard for their function or purpose.

Last but not least, separate yourself from abusive people or circumstances. Anyone who assaults you mentally or physically should not be allowed to have free reign in your life. Get counseling and try to uncover the root of any self-destructive behavior. Do whatever you must to celebrate your life while you still have it. When you abuse yourself, or allow yourself to be abused in any way, you are telling God that you have no love and respect for Him or what He created.

Whatever you do, don't say you can't afford to look beauty-full. When you know Who you are and Who's you are, everything you need will come to you.

The Bible tells us that the beauty-full woman will always be the recipient of blessings.

Ezekiel 35:26 - I will send down showers in season; there will be showers of blessings.

Dueteronomy 28:2 - And all these blessings shall come upon you and overtake you because you obey the voice of the Lord your God.

Verse 3:3 Blessed shall you be in the city. Blessed shall you be in the country.

Verse 3:4 Blessed are the children of your body, and blessed be the increase of your wealth.

Verse 3:6 Blessed shall you be when you come in, and blessed shall you be when you go out.

Verse 3:12 The Lord will open to you His "good treasure." The heavens to give the rain to your land in it's season and all of the works of your hands will be BLESSED.

I join with you as you celebrate the new creation that is being birthed inside of you. Enjoy your new life to the fullest. When I think of you making your grand entrance with your head held high, shining like a star, all I can say is...

"You go girl!"

* * *

Beauty-full

I still have mental images of sitting in front of a worn out
television set with a coat hanger for my antenna
My eyes were glued to the screen as pretty ladies with pretty
hair floated across the stage and disappeared
into the ivory towers.
In their presence I looked up to them and accused them of
looking down on me.
My speech was awkward as I imitated their words and
mimicked their silly gestures.
I tried to be proud of who I was, but their eyes told me, their
words told me, and their world told me they were
more and I was less.
I would have died in my feelings of nothingness, until I
looked into the mirror of God's Word and discovered my real
and beauty-full creation.
For He has drawn my complexion from the richness of the
earth and shaped me in the image of the rolling hillsides.
My wisdom runs deeper than the bottomless ocean and my
spirit is as pure as the mountain streams.
He has given me the heart of a lioness, yet made me
gentle as a dove.
I bend beneath the pressures of life like a grace-full palm tree
dancing with the winds of adversity.
In the arms of the man I love, I am
the sweetness of ripe mango.
My children look to me as their invincible rock of protection.
As I continue to unwrap the gift of my creation, I look to
God with gratitude and thanksgiving.
For I never imagined things so valuable could be placed
inside of such a simple container.

I lift my voice and the nightingale is ashamed
to sing again.
I spread my wings and the eagles flee from the sky as I soar
higher than I could ever imagine.
I think invisible thoughts, and the creativity of my hands
bring them into existence.
Glory and honor bow at my feet, for again and again my
power finds expression and explodes into a million frag-
mented acts of love and kindness.
Joyfully I give the glory and honor back to
my heavenly Father.
For He rescued me from the prison of deception. He has
healed me from the blindness of this world and opened the
eyes of my understanding.
In celebration of my birth and my destiny, he adorns me with
crowns of gold, diamonds, rubies and precious pearls.
For I am more than flesh, more than race, more than gender,
more than culture or nationality.
I am the reflection and the fullness of His glory and
His beauty.
Yes... I am God's gift to the world!
As I give of myself back to Him, the seed of my existence
falls to the ground. I die to self - I am born again to
His plan and purpose.
Indeed I blossom... indeed I bloom... indeed I grow and
flower into a woman full of beauty and Beauty-full.

Bibliography

American Standard Bible
Nelson Publishers

Henry/Clarke/Brown - The Bethany Parallel Commentary -
Bethany House Publishers

Claud Anderson, Ed.D. - Black Labor White Wealth
Duncan & Duncan Publishers

Diane Ackerman - A Natural History Of Love
Random House Publishers

J.C. deGraft-Johnson - African Glory
Black Classic Press

Alton Hornsby, Jr. - Chronology of African-American History - Gale Research, Inc.

Tom Feelings (Introduction by Dr. John Henrik Clarke)
The Middle Passage - Dial Books

LaVerne Powlis - Beauty From The Inside Out
Doubleday Press

Tonya Bolden - African American Women
Adams Media Corporation

Dennis Rodman - Bad As I Wanna Be
Bantam - Doubleday Publishers

Audio Tape Series

001: GOD MADE ME BEAUTY-FULL
Building Self-Esteem In African American Women/$20.00 per set

002: INNER-HEALING
Song of Solomon (building self-esteem), Overcoming Rejection, Guilt, Shame and Forgiveness, How to have a Successful Pity Party/$20.00 per set

003: BUILDING STRONG RELATIONSHIPS
John & Maria (a family crisis), Covenant Relationships (building a strong marriage), Healing the Family Feud, The Family Covenant/$20.00 per set

004: SUCCESS-FULL LIVING SERIES
Doing Business in Deep Waters, The Price of a Dream, Real Success, Superwoman/$20.00 per set

005: SPIRITUAL GROWTH SERIES
Affection Toward God (Building a strong prayer life), Spiritual Warfare, Taking Back what the Enemy has Stolen, Satan's Hunt for Souls/$20.00 per set

006: FOR WOMEN ONLY
Helpmates, Handmaidens and Harlots 1-2, Working Women 1-2, The Virtuous Woman, Daughters of Zion/$20.00 per set

007: SINGLES SERIES
How to Find and Keep Your Man, God's Plan for Intimacy 1-2, The Sexual Revolution, Single Parenting/$20.00 per set

Additional Book Orders

God Made Me Beauty-full, Building Self-Esteem In African American Women $12.00 ea.

* * *

If you would like information on speaking engagements, workshops, or other programs by Terri McFaddin, or to order additional books and tapes, please write or call: Terri McFaddin, c/o Harvest Enterprises, 686 Arroyo Parkway, Suite 174, Pasadena, CA 91105; (888) 379-5907

Please include $2.00 shipping and handling/$1.00 each additional product.